SERIOUS SURVEILLANCE *FOR THE* PRIVATE INVESTIGATOR

SERIOUS SURVEILLANCE

Bob Bruno

SURVEILLANCE

FOR THE PRIVATE

INVESTIGATOR

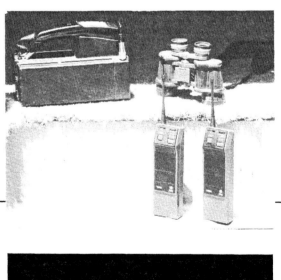

Serious Surveillance for the Private Investigator
by Bob Bruno

Copyright © 1992 by Bob Bruno

ISBN 0-87364-665-7
Printed in the United States of America

Published by Paladin Press, a division of
Paladin Enterprises, Inc., P.O. Box 1307,
Boulder, Colorado 80306, USA.
(303) 443-7250

Direct inquiries and/or orders to the above address.

PALADIN, PALADIN PRESS, and the "horse head" design
are trademarks belonging to Paladin Enterprises and
registered in United States Patent and Trademark Office.

Visit our Web site at www.paladin-press.com

TABLE OF CONTENTS

Page

CHAPTER 1:   Why Surveillance?   1

CHAPTER 2:   Getting Information   6

CHAPTER 3:   Getting Into Position, and STAYING There!   15

CHAPTER 4:   Your Professional Surveillance Vehicle   18

CHAPTER 5:   Video and Photo Equipment & Accessories   27

CHAPTER 6:   Communications   43

CHAPTER 7:   Keeping Comfortable   49

CHAPTER 8:   Security   55

CHAPTER 9:   Are You a Surveillance "Player," or Are You Just Playing
             Games?   57

CHAPTER 10: Teaming   60

CHAPTER 11: Creativity   63

CHAPTER 12: Over-Creativity   70

CHAPTER 13: How Cobra Does It   75

CHAPTER 14: Privacy, Invasion Thereof   79

CHAPTER 15: The Report   82

Appendix: Cobra Company Order and Report Forms   85

About the Author   87

DISCLAIMER

Some of the concepts and surveillance techniques discussed in this book, while acceptable in the part of the Southwest where Cobra Company does business, may be unethical or illegal in you part of the country. *Use Caution!*

We do not advocate the use of any of the methods disclosed in this book. If an idea discussed herein is used within your own business, we recommend you alter it, if necessary, so that it is *entirely legal* within your locale. When a technique used in PI surveillance work puts you in that gray area between right and wrong, you quickly find yourself *in the wrong,* and in trouble with the law, your subjects, and your clients. We assume *no responsibility* for your use--or misuse--of the techniques discussed in this book.

Once again, it is not the intent of the author to suggest, promote, or recommend your use of any of the concepts discussed in this book in the course of conducting your business. The purpose of this book is to show you how we at Cobra Company conduct...

SERIOUS SURVEILLANCE

PREFACE

This book is about the nuts and bolts, the science and art, and the *details*, of taking covert photographs and video tapes of individuals who do things that are either immoral, illegal, or just not right.

I will attempt to go into as much detail as possible over every area involved when doing serious surveillance work. It should be noted, however, that some of the things covered in this book might be considered illegal where you live and work. So, it probably would be in your best interest to keep the details of this book to yourself. If you find it interesting or useful, don't give it to your associates; tell them to buy their own copy. I can use the money.

While some of the techniques discussed in this book are, strictly speaking, illegal, careful attention to the details and a lot of practice in their proper implementation may make them borderline legal, if somewhat shady. And, as I'll discuss further on, there are times (like when you want to protect your family), when doing things to the letter of the law *just won't cut it*.

In my 25 years of involvement in different types of investigation work, I personally find surveillance to be the most interesting and certainly the most lucrative. During that time I have never, anywhere, been able to find a book that tells me exactly how it is on the street, and the equipment or tools I will need to get the job done, in quite the manner I am about to explain on the following pages. I am sure you will find reading this book to be as interesting as I found writing it to be.

> **A NOTE ABOUT GENDER**
> Some of the best investigators I know are women. And not all the subjects we do surveillance on are men. However, for the sake of simplicity, I'm going to use male gender terminology in this book, except in specific instances where female gender is appropriate. So if you get tired of "he" and "him", get creative in your mind...

CHAPTER 1: Why Surveillance?

At one time or another during your career as a Private Investigator, you may be called upon to do surveillance. The person calling about a surveillance job should immediately merit your attention because more than likely that person will be an *insurance adjustor* representing a large firm. Why should that capture your attention?

Consider this: *The largest companies in the world are insurance companies.* They are pleasant and professional to work with, and you, with the proper training and equipment, can supply them with a very valuable service.

More and more, insurance companies are turning to private investigators to provide intense, long-term surveillance on some of their more suspicious claims. Claims which arise out of auto accidents and worker's compensation claims are what serious surveillance is primarily about. In our state (New Mexico), worker's compensation is available for about 660 weeks (12 years) to a maximum of $300.00 per week. Not much to live on, but that's our law. Its purpose is to encourage people to go back to work as soon as medically possible and to discourage them from trying to make a living off the state's checkbook.

THE DISABILITY INSURANCE SCAM

So, how come so many people seem to live prosperous lives while subsisting on worker's compensation proceeds? Here's a recent situation — one we have run into on more than one occasion:

> An adjustor calls our office to 'look into' the activities of a certain individual. I obtain the information needed to do a proper investigation, create a file on the subject, and assign the case to one of the investigators.

> The investigator does a pre-surveillance spot check by checking over the area via a drive-by inspection. He finds out a number of things and returns to the office to consult with the other investigators and to plan his strategy.

> We sit down and begin discussing the things he saw. He notes the

residence appeared to be nearly new, worth about $100,000; with a two car garage and a 30 foot motor home next to the garage. Parked in the driveway was a new pickup sitting next to a new Pontiac Grand Am. (The 19 foot boat was in the back yard!)

LET'S TRY AND FIGURE THIS OUT.

House Payment @ 10% interest	$1,000.00 per month
Motor Home - $60,000 @	363.00 per month
Grand Am - $16,000 @	300.00 per month
Pickup Truck	262.00 per month
Boat and Trailer	189.00 per month
TOTAL OUTLAY	**$2,114.00 per month**

Now his total compensation income is $1,200.00 per month. The above obligations do not include phone, electricity, heat/air conditioning, food, clothing, or any emergency funds. How can he live on $1,200.00 per month? To make matters worse, the subject and his wife were seen on the covered front porch (during the spot check) drinking ice tea (real tough life, huh?). He wasn't working, his wife obviously wasn't working. Surveillance began several days later and some interesting things were learned from the time spent. The subject opened his curtains around 9:30 a.m. every morning, had lunch (on a side patio), and watched television all day.!

Frustrated, our investigator goes back later that night. The investigator's reports throughout the night show the subject going to bed at 10:30 p.m. It begins to appear as though the subject really is bonafide. The investigator finishes the case and begins putting the report together when I stopped him.

We begin discussing the case and the general consensus is maybe a *Paper Trail* should be undertaken. My investigator agrees to take up this task and begin the next day. By noon the next day, the picture begins to come clear.

The subject had purchased disability insurance with the purchases of the house, motor home, car, truck, and boat, which insurance kicked in the day the subject got hurt on his job. (Remember when you got that car loan, and they asked you if you wanted accident or life insurance? It wasn't mandatory for the loan so you probably didn't take it. *Our subject did.*) To further matters, he had a separate accident/disability policy that paid him *$3000.00 a month*! The picture was very clear now. His entire scenario was planned to a tee! What a scam! *Everything was being paid for and it was more profitable to stay home than go to work!* **Neat plan**.

To keep this little scam going, on every doctor's appointment, the subject seemed to get worse and worse. It got to the point where he stated to the doctor he couldn't walk over 100 feet (legs would go numb) or carry anything over 5 pounds. The subject was smart, maybe too smart, in creating a deteriorating condition in order to keep all disability payments continuing to flow in.

My investigator becomes more motivated and determined than ever. One Monday morning around 6:00 a.m., under the cover of darkness, my investigator slips into the neighborhood. He waits. Around 7:45 a.m., the electric garage door opens. My investigator begins recording on video. There is the subject, a full 30 gallon garbage bag in each hand, carrying them to the curb. He places them on the ground, returns to the garage, grabs two more and returns to the curb again! The whole video takes 72 seconds, *but what a video!* He has now documented the subject breaking his lifting restriction. Twenty minutes later, the subject and wife exit the garage in their pickup truck. The investigator follows, *picking up the garbage bags before leaving the area.*

He catches up to the subject and discovers him going to the grocery store. The subject walks 75 yards from his truck to the front door of the store. The investigator follows on foot into the store, one of the "superstores" that carries just about everything. Each aisle is 60 yards long (180 feet). *The subject (who claims to be unable to walk more than 100 feet at a time) . walks 12 aisles.* As the subject is leaving, the investigator high-tails it for his van. He begins filming the subject walking out, pushing the grocery cart.

The surveillance ends.

The video eventually makes it to the doctor's office for viewing. Several days later, the subject is released to work. His compensation is stopped; all the other disability policies abruptly stop. The rest, as they say, is history. Justice prevails and our subject finally gets a job. Not what he wants, but a job. Perseverance pays off. Thousands of dollars have been saved-over some garbage! And some Serious Surveillance.

Needless to say, the insurance company has become one of our most loyal customers!

PERSONAL INJURY & "DOUBLE-DIPPING"

Let's take the previous scenario and give a slight twist:

Our subject is a district manager of a small chain of three shoe stores. While traveling (in his own vehicle) from one store to check on his other stores, he gets into an accident (no physical signs of injury) which is the other guy's fault. Same house, same car, same truck, same boat, and same motor home.

His neck gets stiff and he goes to the hospital to get it checked out. The doctors say, "Stay home a few days and rest. You'll be okay in a few days. If not, see the doctor on the referral card."

He goes home and decides that he likes his time off. His neck does feel better but..."Well, I'm not ready to go back to work." Several month go by, his worker's compensation is paying *two-thirds of his salary* (it happened on the job) *and his medical bills.*

He photocopies his medical bills, which by now have gotten quite large, and takes them to his insurance company *which also pays on his medical pay coverage up to $50,000.00 with no deductible.* Just present the bills. No questions asked, regardless of whose fault it was!

This is called "double-dipping." It's common practice for the smart "professional" claimant. Not only is the possibility high of getting a good compensation settlement, but suing the other driver's auto insurance is a sure thing and with exceptionally good prospects of getting a large settlement from it also!

What's needed?

SERIOUS SURVEILLANCE

This is what this book is all about. Whether the surveillance is fixed-position, afoot, mobile, by helicopter, from a tree, apartment, foxhole, or a hill behind a fence, do whatever the situation requires, but do something! You may be the last person to help. Now, let's get on to the real techniques and equipment we use to go about doing serious surveillance.

CHAPTER 2:   Getting Information

The interesting thing I have found over the years, no matter where I go, is how many *contacts*, or information sources, most investigators have. Police on TV call their information sources "snitches." I guess using contacts for information gathering gives some people a feeling of power. It is "secret" knowledge that only you have from your "secret contact." Frankly, most of the information needed in our business is available at minimal or no cost through various government agencies (federal, state, county, and local, as well as privately owned utilities). This information is available due to the Freedom of Information Act.

You, as an investigator, should not let anyone hinder your efforts in trying to obtain necessary information. Occasionally, you will run into an entry-level clerk who'll try, out of ignorance or simple malice to give you a hard time. "I can't give out any of that information." Your reply should be confident and quick. "I thought that was available due to the Freedom of Information Act!" Being a minimum wage employee, odds are he won't know what to do and will more than likely give you the necessary information to lesson any embarrassment on his part.

We're going to discuss here, and elsewhere, another technique for gathering information. We call it **Methods**. No matter where you go, who you talk to, what you want to know or even why you want to know it, if you use our Methods or develop your own Methods, you'll find you'll be able to get a job done without relying directly on 'Contacts'. You'll get better information. You should use our Methods only as guidelines, from which you can develop your own Methods. But first, a couple of reasons for *NOT relying heavily on "contacts."*

RISK

> We have found that contacts often stick their necks out for you when they reveal sensitive information. Sometimes, they put their jobs on the line for you. Would you be able to sleep well knowing you got someone fired just because a friend revealed the address off a confidential list? Something he wasn't supposed to reveal?

RELIABILITY

So much for those contacts. Some contacts transfer, some move, some die, some retire from their work. An emergency arises and you need the information and you need information, only to find out your contact is no longer there for whatever reason. What do you do? Time is of the essence and you don't have time to go somewhere and make friends with someone.

Sure, surveillance investigators, at one time or another, have to make physical contact with another person or place to get necessary information. However, it is virtually impossible to have *contacts* everywhere. And we've already discussed some reasons for not relying on contacts. So, a basic requirement for all investigators is that they know how to **skip trace** or how to locate people-where to go and who to talk to. To begin a proper surveillance, pre-investigate work must be done so that when the investigation does begin you are watching the right individual.

Your journey may begin at the County Assessor's office to determine if the subject owns a home. Sometimes, looking right under your nose might produce the results you are after. *Try the phone book.* Call directory assistance, or the utilities.

We have found the utilities to be an excellent source of information. Due to the system used in our country, *even if the utilities were to read the following Method*, it would be difficult for them to change their procedures.

This is one of the areas I was telling you about where it may be on the verge of illegal to use this Method, so *I don't recommend it.* But here it is anyway, *just for your entertainment...*

PHONE COMPANY SCENARIO

Let's say you have a person's name and phone number, possibly a social security number, maybe a date of birth. Call the phone company, temporarily assume that individual's identity, and the call may go something like this:

"This is Julie. Can I help you?"

Practice and you can get this right. If you don't believe me try your own phone with your own number.

> "Yes, ummm, Julie. I can't find my phone bill. Have you been mailing it to my box number or my house?"

> "What is your name and number, sir?"

Again, since you are assuming the identity of the individual you are looking for, remember to tell her the right name.

> "Yes, my name is (subject's name), and my number is (subject's number)."

> "Thank you, sir. Hold on please."

She brings it up her computer, notes that the name and number match, and says:

> "Well, sir, I show your bill is going to 1330 Main Street. It was mailed out. Haven't you received it?"

> "My wife could have paid it and not told me. I guess I'll check with her."

> "All right, sir. If we can be of further service, feel free to call back."

Practice this until you get it down smoothly. Don't slip up or hesitate because the slightest hesitation may make the representative suspicious. She may then ask you for your mother's maiden name, or something equally disastrous—especially if things go wrong before she gives you the address. Have all your answers down pat before they are asked, so if they are asked, you'll have the answer.

> **Potential Problem #1:** The phone company inputs this call into its computers and stores it for up to three month. If you subject makes any inquiry during that time he may be told "Did you get your mail straightened out?" Can you imagine the look on your subject's face when he hears that? He has no idea what she's talking about.

Potential Problem #2: The representative may get suspicious, not press you for further information, hang up on you, and call the subject on the phone to find out if he just inquired about his phone bill. The risk is that this might tip the subject off about potential surveillance, especially if the representative tells him, "All I gave out was your address, sir." That's exactly what he didn't want given out.

Here are a couple of hints for minimizing potential problems:

1.   Call during their busiest time of day and week. Odds are in your favor they"ll tell you quickly so they can get on to their next call.

2.   If you can't call during the busiest time of day or week, call just before the business office closes. (I love our system!)

        Another thing you may want to keep in mind is that this works for unlisted, unpublished numbers also. If you want a *guarantee this will work,* have a female call. Our experience has been it always works. Every time.

NOTE: How to make yourself (and Your Family) Invisible!

This brings up an interesting point. You probably have your name and your number listed in the phone book the way most investigators list their numbers: "Kevin Jones, Private Invesigator.......555-7575." What's to prevent your subject or anyone else from tracking you down? Most investigators loathe individuals knowing where they are. Here's a way to get around that. It costs a few dollars, but it is well worth the price especially if someone nasty pays you a visit where you live or work because you don't use it.

❑   Dream up an alias name − nothing radical, something you can remember − and get phone service in that name. If you default in a few months, they'll come after you for intent to defraud by using a false name. However if you default after several years of paying your bills timely, no big deal. There was no intent to defraud. Just make arrangements with the phone company to pay up. By the way, have your bills mailed to a P.O. Box.

❏   To further protect you, give the service representatives a code. Tell the service representatives that they are not to give out any information to anyone for any reason unless the caller comes up with the code. You can use the last four digits of your social security number, a favorite color, an animal or whatever. BUT, remember your code name or number because they won't tell you squat until you get past that code, regardless of what you tell them. Don't tell anyone your code. No one. This locks out everybody.

❏   You now have a different name, a listed number, no listed address, no traceable unlisted number charges and a code to prevent anyone from locating you. Not even the police or the federal government, even with a court order to the phone company to release your number, can find it because it's not in your name. It's safe. It works. It can also get you in trouble, so practice it before you do it. Remember, being a private investigator is like being an actor. Act it out, and you'll succeed.

GAS OR ELECTRIC UTILITIES

The gas company or electric company operate on a different system. *Pay attention.* When you call these utilities, the first thing they'll ask you for is your account number. *You don't usually have that even when you call for your own home.* Since you don't know your account number she'll ask you your address. *That's what you want to know in the first place.* Since you don't know that either, it appears you have now come to a dead end. Not so.

After practicing the following, you'll be amazed. (If you don't practice, and do it wrong, you'll be amazed all right, *but in the wrong way!*)

The conversation must go something like this:

"Hello, this is your local gas/electric company."

"Hello, my name is (subjects name), and since the first of the year I've rented out all my properties. The tenants were supposed to have put the gas/electric in their names. However, the other day I was speaking to one of my tenants, I can't remember which one now, but I was hoping you could look up my name and see if the tenant has put the service in his name yet."

Most representatives will not be clear on exactly what you want. Tell them there should be only two properties in *subject's name.*

"...one where I live and the other belonging to the tenant."

So, by the process of elimination she should find the address by name with no problem. Of course she'll find only one and that will be the subject's address.

Play it up and say, "Oh yes, now I remember. I did have them put it in their name. Thanks anyway."

HANG UP.

You now have found a way to get an address through the gas or electric company. This also works with the cable TV company (assuming the subject has cable). Usually, just a name and phone number will do.

These are just some of the ways to get information. Modify these Methods for your own area, then add new ones that fit.

THE RADIO STATION "MONEY-CALL"

I've saved my favorite for last. Over the last several years, radio stations have been giving away money to get the public's attention. They are competing fiercely against each other.

You can benefit from this fierce competition. Puzzled? If you have the subject's name and his telephone number, that should be all you need to:

A: Find out if who you are calling is the subject.

B: Determine that he is actually living "*there*" and where "*there*" is.

Radio Station disc jockeys deepen their voice, speak with complete clarity, control the conversation and airways, and are very dominant. Try this ruse on a friend. Deepen your voice, call him on the phone, turn on your radio so that it can be heard in the background, just as if you were a D.J. in a sound booth, and in a fairly commanding voice, say.....

"WHAT'S YOUR FAVORITE RADIO STATION?"

At this point he usually won't believe his ears and will blurt out to, "...repeat that again." He'll get hyper, maybe hysterical, but you will have his full attention.

If he hesitates, tell him:

"YOU'VE GOT TEN SECONDS TO TELL ME YOUR FAVORITE RADIO STATION."

You may get a "Who is this?" with a smile in his voice, not knowing whether to believe you or not. But you will be able to tell they want to believe this call is real.

So let it be real. Play along.

About this time he will say KRTR (or whatever station in your area is popular for that age group).

Regardless of what he says, make up another radio station call letter sign.

Tell him he missed out on a whole pot of money, but *for being a good sport and trying to guess, you're going to give him lunch for two at* (pick a restaurant).

Gently get into the conversation. If it's a woman, it might go something like this:

"WHO AM I SPEAKING TO?"

"My name's Linda, Linda Wilson."

"WELL HELLO, LINDA WILSON, DO YOU HAVE A BOYFRIEND OR HUSBAND YOU WANT TO TAKE ALONG WITH YOU?"

"Well, yes, my husband."

"ARE YOU GOING TO TELL HIM ABOUT THE POT OF MONEY YOU ALMOST WON?"

"No, he'd kill me."

"WELL LINDA, WHAT DO YOU DO FOR A LIVING?"

"I'm a nightshift nurse at St. Vincent's hospital."

"WELL, THAT'S GREAT, LINDA. I HOPE YOU ENJOY YOUR LUNCH! IN ABOUT 4-6 WEEKS, YOU WILL HAVE TWO TICKETS DELIVERED TO YOU, AND ALL YOU HAVE TO DO IS SHOW I.D. WE SUBCONTRACT OUT OUR DELIVERIES AND TO KEEP THEM HONEST WE HAVE YOU SIGN FOR IT, SO WE KNOW YOU GOT THE TICKETS.

"My husband won't believe this!"

"WHERE SHOULD WE DELIVER THESE TICKETS TO, LINDA?"

"Well (hesitation), to my home at 1218 Vista Street."

"LINDA, IT'S BEEN GOOD TALKING WITH YOU. YOU'VE BEEN A GOOD SPORT. THANKS FOR TALKING WITH US!"

Hang up.....

This will take a little practice, but it works and works great. It's simple and quick. You catch them off guard and they are more likely to say things without thinking. In 4-6 weeks they will have forgotten what station called them or that they were even called.

If you feel guilty, get a gift certificate for two made out from that radio station (the one you made up), and have it delivered and signed for. Easy on the conscience.

Some other things you can learn from this:

> If the subject is on worker's compensation, for example off work from an auto accident, you just found out not only that *he is working* when he isn't supposed to be able to do so, but also *where he's working* and *when he's working.*

When doing this, do it in a room where you will not be distracted, not have any witnesses, and make sure you have on some mellow rock and roll or whatever is popular in your area.

If you live in a small town, improvise. It will take practice but after about 4 or 5 times you'll get it down.

Practice and assume the identity of the D.J.

It'll come to you.

CHAPTER 3: Getting Into Position, and STAYING There!

Now that you know who your subject is and where he lives, you need to know what his activities are. Do not, repeat, *DO NOT* blatantly drive past the subject's house back and forth looking for a place to do surveillance. You'll attract too much attention.

First get a map and review the area. Look at all the streets around the subject's residence. Learn their names and exits in case a pursuit is necessary or in case two investigators are needed. After you are familiar with the area, do a drive-by with another investigator in a nonsurveillance car (but one that won't attract attention). Let your partner quickly survey the area for a surveillance spot, while you drive, or vice versa. This way you won't draw a lot of neighborhood attention by stopping and looking around.

For simplicity, we'll speak in terms of city surveillance.

You won't always find a park or business parking lot where you can place your vehicle. More than likely (if your luck is like mine) your subject will live smack in the middle of the neighborhood.

If this is the case, here's what to do: park your vehicle at least 3-4 homes from your subject's. Go up to the door of the house you park in front of, whip out your private investigator's I.D. or business card, and tell them this (modify for your style):

> "Hello, sir. My name is Kevin Jones and I am a private investigator. My partner and I have been tracking down a little thirteen year old runaway for about six months, and we believe she's living down the street with a male who is giving her refuge. She's about this high (raise your hand to about your chin) has brown hair, kind of thin, answers to the name of Lisa and we have been hired by the mother to see to it that she gets home."

At this point you will have elicited sympathy. Play it up. Keep up the story.

> They will more than likely ask what they can do or even start pointing out where she could be living, because they might have seen unknown females

in the neighborhood lately. Wherever they point, tell them, don't point or look around, that no, they are in the other direction. (Opposite from where your subject is.) Tell them that all you have to do is take pictures of this little girl, air-express them back to her home town (make up one), and if that's the girl, you'll turn the rest of the photos over to the authorities. Explain it is necessary that they tell no one since the P.I. business is so glorified that word will get around quickly. To have a PRIVATE INVESTIGATOR right in front of their house is incredible looking for a poor runaway no less.

Explain: "...they usually get abused at home or think that they got a raw deal and now are afraid to go home. We simply have to take pictures, if they are not the right girl, we'll have to come back."

You might continue with an explanation that, as a Private Investigator, the law says you can park on any street at any time (unless it says no parking, of course), but since you're going to right out in front of their house, you thought you would be courteous and tell them what you are doing. Also explain that if the runaway sees a police car cruise slowly by the house, she might run and *"...we wouldn't want that to happen, would we?"* This will keep them from calling the police. (You don't need to be visited by the police. They will blow your cover.)

What you are trying to do is look like you belong in the neighborhood. Do this in the early evening while there is still light out. Don't be afraid to look your neighbor right in the eye. Eye contact is important. Practice your story. You'll find you will become quick friends with this neighbor and he may even allow you to park in his driveway or yard. You would be surprised what some people will do to help you. Once a lady brought us ice tea to our vehicle. Needless to say, this didn't help our cover much, but we took the tea anyway.

Practice your story. Get "Missing Person" posters and memorize what's on them.

The results are amazing. This Method has worked for us every time we have used it.

There are some times when we get to do surveillance from a park, from an apartment, from a commercial parking lot, such as a grocery store parking lot. You name it, we've been there. We've even been in fox holes, on top of buildings, in the woods, in the mountains and have done pursuits in airplanes. You'll learn to be creative. We've even spotchecked areas on bicycles.

Once you are in position, *do not move.* Stay put for the entire day or until *at least one hour after your surveillance has been completed.* Sometimes another neighbor will be watching you just to see who *you* are watching. If you take off right after the subject does, they'll know who you are doing surveillance on, and your cover will be blown.

> ❑   The hard part of surveillance is staying put. Whom ever you are doing surveillance on, you're doing it because the subject may have something to hide. To determine if you are watching him, he may leave to see if you follow. Chances are he's just driving around the block or to the local 7-11 store. If that's the case, and you roar off in pursuit, you've blown your cover. If necessary, stay put, radio (equipment is discussed later) to a partner and have him follow the subject. Your vehicle stays put.

Good investigators become successful investigators through patience. The longer you can sit there and do surveillance the more comfortable everyone in the neighborhood will feel. The subject will be convinced you are not watching him. The more patient you become, the more successful you will be in getting the subject on video.

The more good video you take on any subject, the more your credibility will grow. Good credibility means "good reputation," and you will soon see clients wanting you to do work for them.

Too many investigators turn in lengthy reports with no photos or video. Most don't have video cameras anyway. These are the ones who aren't in the surveillance business long, or who ruin it for those of us who are truly professionals. Actually, these are the people we hope will read this book.

CHAPTER 4: Your Professional Surveillance Vehicle

For surveillance many investigators use automobiles of any make, model, year and color. In most neighborhoods it is totally impractical to do surveillance in a car. Our company philosophy is that the ultimate professional surveillance vehicle is a *van*. An effective surveillance vehicle should be:

- ☐ Invisible – an unremarkable color that no one remembers clearly.

- ☐ A model that is hard to identify, both on the street and in court, and easily confused with other makes. ("I think it was a Chevy van, but it could have been a Dodge, they all look so much alike.)

- ☐ Well equipped and well organized. If you can't take video or photos on a minute's notice, why are you doing surveillance in the first place?

- ☐ Comfortable. You may need to spend 16 hours or more inside that vehicle, to get 30 seconds worth of damaging evidence.

From bumper to bumper, no part of the van is overlooked when considering it for surveillance.

COLOR:
Many colors won't work. Two-tone colored vans are not acceptable. Acceptable colors are mostly *low-key, everyday earthtones*: browns, tans, grays, off-white, or very pale blue (almost silver).

Reds, greens, yellows, blacks, etc., are not acceptable.

STYLE:
Usually a converted cargo van is best to start with. Have the van totally insulated with a plywood floor covered with low-pile carpeting for sound insulation. It is best that the van have two windows in the rear doors that open and to windows on the sides, towards the rear. The rear door windows should not be tinted. The side windows, which should be glass, not plastic, and

flat, should be tinted. Curtains should be placed on the windows the color of the van and a curtain directly behind the front seats should be installed on a track on the ceiling.

ACCESSORIES:

There are two accessories your van should have. One is an auxiliary power system. For about $180.00 a battery isolator can be installed *(See Figure 1)*. This extra battery will power your camera equipment for a solid 48 hours without a recharge. When the engine is running, the front battery is supplying the rear battery with recharging power. This lets you avoid starting the vehicle while on surveillance.

The other accessory to have is wooden camera case bolted to the floor to hold your camera equipment. This case should be about 15 inches deep, 40 inches long and about 4 inches from the ceiling. It should have doors with locks. It should have compartments to hold various pieces of equipment. The cost of having this piece of equipment made is around three hundred fifty dollars.

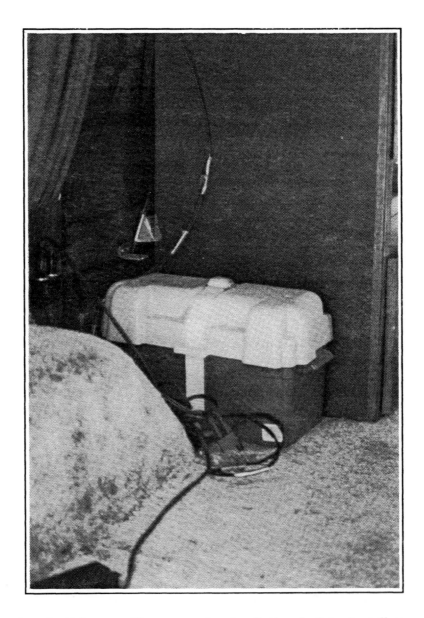

Figure 1. Interior of a Cobra surveillance van, showing Battery Isolator installation.

Figure 2. Wooden Camera & Equipment Case should have locking doors, lots of compartments.

Now, what NOT to have (see Figures 3 & 4):

- ❏   no racks

- ❏   no ladders

- ❏   no spare tires on the exterior

- ❏   no antennas other than AM/FM

- ❏   no running boards

- ❏   no bumper stickers

- ❏   no sign of any kind

❑   no vehicle insignias

❑   take off the Ford, Dodge or Chevy chrome insignias

❑   take it all off, fill the holes and repaint the van.

❑   incidentally, repaint the van to an earthtone color.

Figure 3. This is a typical surveillance van used in our company. Note the lack of insignias, racks, ladders, spare tires, or anything else making the vehicle identifiable. Note the lack of any antennas, except for am/fm.

Figure 4. This is the front of the same van. Note the only antenna is the am/fm antenna. Dodge insignia has been removed from the front. No bumper stickers or insignias or anything remain to identify this vehicle.

If You are Stopped by the Police

When a rookie completes a police academy, his first shift assignment is usually from 11 P.M. to 7 A.M. for several years. This gives him more respect for the job. Not too many people are running around town after midnight, compared to the daytime hours. After several years of this, if he's proceeding on course, his next shift will be the Swing Shift, from 3:00 P.M. to 11 P.M.

Here, the officer is introduced to more traffic, evening rush hour traffic and late night drunks. On this shift he is introduced to the most dangerous people and high-risk action.

After working successfully at this shift he will eventually work from 7:00 A.M.

to 3:00 P.M. He is now a seasoned officer, and situations which might panic a rookie have become old-hat.

> If an officer is called to check out your suspicious van, he may stay three to four car lengths away while running your plate. Now remember, you are in an anonymous van with no markings, curtains closed and a current sticker on your plate. He hears over his radio "There's no record on that plate." The seasoned officer (who is most likely to be on duty) would know this is an undercover vehicle (or it wouldn't have a *current tag*), start his vehicle and do one of two things.

☐   First, and from our experience most commonly, he would place his patrol car in reverse and get the devil out of there, as he may think he might have just blown his own undercover agents' cover;

☐   Second, he may just pass by slowly to pacify whatever neighbor called in to report a suspicious vehicle. Which brings us to an important point, what to do...

In the event you are pulled over while in pursuit of someone, *stay in the vehicle*. Forget about your subject. He's long gone. *Forget it*, deal with the matter at hand. The officer is approaching a vehicle that he knows there is no record on, has its window obscured by curtains (see *Figure 7*), and is just an all-around suspicious-looking vehicle (to a police officer). All he can think about is that he is entering a blind area, by himself, while there may be several people in the vehicle with large guns. This has happened before to police officers, and anyone would be a bit apprehensive in approaching the vehicle.

Make sure, before he even gets out of his patrol car, that you immediately put both hands on the steering wheel. *Do not hesitate,* because as easily as you can see the officer in your side mirror, he can see you. If you are messing around trying to get your license out or any other movement not consistent with calmness, you may find this officer will have several of his friends completely surrounding your vehicle. Keep your hands on the steering wheel and let the officer speak first.

After he does greet you, (he'll do so from over your left shoulder), if you were speeding, (more than likely you were) tell him the truth. You are an investigator in pursuit of a subject. He may ask to see your identification. If he does, *take one hand only off the wheel and reach for your license* (P.I. License) and show it to him. At this point he should have calmed down, and tell you, "O.K. I understand, but try to keep your speed down." Normally he'll drive away.

Figure 5. Curtains (shown drawn, per surveillance procedures), can look suspicious to an approaching officer...

Remember, he's a seasoned officer, not to be bluffed or lied to. Tell the truth. He may even help you. He might even run the subject's plate for you, but more than likely he will probably apologize for pulling you over, but due to your speed and no record on your tags he had to stop you. With a good attitude, you'll be on your way in a few minutes. Easy. *With a good attitude on your part.*

Getting pulled over, unfortunately, is unavoidable and does sometimes happen. If handled properly, it's just part of the job and can actually

improve your relationship with the police. Handled improperly?
Well...remember these officers can take your freedom away *right now*, even
if only temporarily, and that can mess up your whole day. It's not worth it.

CHAPTER 5: Video and Photo Equipment & Accessories

Let's go on to more of the nuts and bolts necessary to being a successful surveillance investigator.

You now have a fully useful van out of which to work.

> Remember:
> If you are using a van, say in Phoenix, you'll more than likely need to worry about heat stroke. But, if you use a van in upstate Maine you'll need to prepare it for extreme cold. Use your head and adapt your vehicle to fit your area. You will find that extreme temperatures will also affect the operation of your camera equipment.

VIDEO

Figure 6. Panasonic PV465, with 4X Extender Mounted.

Our company uses the Panasonic PV645, a 12-power camcorder with an attachable 4-times extender (See *Figure 6*)

We have two in the company and one 8-power camera. We chose this over a
professional mini-cam, like the TV stations use, for several reasons:

❑   First of all, our camcorders use a VHS tape, versus the mini-cam's
         more expensive "BETAcam" commercial format. When we finish
         video taping our subject, we take the video out, stick it in a case and
         send it to our client's attorney, if an attorney has been engaged at
         that point; if not it goes directly to the client. In either case, no
         editing, no copying, no duplicating, no tampering. Most of our
         clients have, or have access to, a VHS VCR and can play our tape
         immediately. Once they review it, they usually give it to their
         attorney. Once in his hands, the evidence is protected from
         opposing counsel.

         The lawyer is an officer of the court, which expects the lawyer to act
         within the law. If the investigator holds the tape until court time, you
         can bet the opposing counsel will not ask the attorney if he tampered
         with the tape in any way; he will not ask the client; he will not ask any
         witnesses. However, you can be assured he will ask YOU the
         questions. The questioning can go like this:

         "Mr. Jones, did you take this video on my client?"

         "Yes, I did."

         "Did you at anytime edit this tape for any reason?"

         "No."

         "Did you at any time see the subject and not film him?"

         "No."

         "Did you in any way tamper with this tape?"

         "Well, I was asked to duplicate it by my client."

"If that were the case, isn't it true that your client could have easily said, leave that last part off, just erase it, and you would have done that too?"

"No, I WOULDN'T HAVE DONE THAT!""

"Why, Mr. Jones (raised eyebrows and a sneer on the upper lip), didn't you just testify that you were asked to duplicate the tape in question and you admitted you did? What would prevent you from tampering, altering, editing, erasing this video tape?"

The best way to prevent this from happening is to make sure the attorney representing your client gets the tape immediately. Once you have been tagged as having tampered with evidence, even though duplicating a tape was harmless, the tag will stay with you and your client list will go down. So much for your P.I. business. So much for your credibility.

❏   Another reason for choosing this camera over a mini-cam is technology. Every year, it seems that manufacturers are inventing newer and more powerful cameras that do more things: batteries, that last longer, lenses that are more powerful, accessories that override the lens to open and close the iris (to be able to shoot in the shadows of someone's porch, or to adjust if too much light is coming in). Frankly, it costs less to upgrade to the latest technology, if you start with a lower cost in the first place.

In fairness, the obvious advantage of the "professional" mini-cam is that it comes with a C-or-T mount lens capability. This means that you can fit virtually any 35mm camera lens on your industrial-strength mini-cam. The immediate effects are wonderful. After some time though, it will begin to show some wear at the mount. Removing and changing lenses wear out the mount and soon you will have a very loose lens to deal with on your camera. Also, just like consumer-grade products, in one year, this camera will be obsolete.

❑   Our PV645 camcorder cost us $1,195.00 and a professional minicam
       goes from $7,000 to $15,000. So if both cameras do the same
       things, except you can change lenses on the mini-cam (but have to
       add an extender to the camcorder), you will probably come to same
       conclusion we did: it is not worth the extra several thousand dollars
       extra for the "Big Gun." At least, that's our experience.

With the way electronic equipment is changing and constantly upgraded, modified,
and improved upon, we are continuously changing our own equipment.

CAMCORDER TIP

Our camcorder has a 1.5 second operation delay (which is typical), from the time it's
turned on. Get used to this delay, and practice adapting to it in your surveillance. If
you're not sure why this is critical...

...go down the street, tell your wife to take the garbage to the curb (if you
live in an area where they do that) and watch how quickly it is done...just
on a normal basis. Tell her not to hurry; just have her do it normally, at
usual speed. You'll be surprised at first when all you can get on film is her
reaching for the front door to enter the house. Why? Because by the
time your brain reacts to what your eyes see, several seconds have
passed by. By the time your camera is powered up, another second and
a half has passed by, and by the time the camera is actually recording,
another second or two has passed. Thus, the only thing you have on
video is the back side of your wife entering the house.

The scenario could be the same if the wife were a subject who had a bad
back from a car accident and was told not to lift more than 5 pounds by her
doctor; and you didn't get that little episode on film. **Allowing for that 1.5
second delay is critical,** but with patience and practice you will be able to
do it.

TRIPODS & DOLLYS

With the camcorder you must always strive to get the best video possible. That means no zooming in and out and a steady hold on the camera. Lots of zooming in and out tends to make a viewer nauseous.

Figure 7. Tiltall Tripod mounted on standard Tripod Dolly.   *Figure 8. Tripod & Dolly with mounted Camcorder.*

To get steady video a strong tripod is necessary. If you hold it on your shoulder, you're going to get "interesting" results. When your subject comes into view, doing something they ought not to be doing, and you see it, especially after having waited for several hours or longer, the camcorder goes up on the shoulder, your breathing gets heavier, the camera starts to go up and down with your breathing and the end result cannot be ignored. Bad video. Some viewers might even get seasick from the up and down motion of the picture.

On a tripod, the camcorder is pointed out the window and ready to run. Simply flip on the power switch and begin recording. Turn the camera gently as the individual begins to move. Now, if the subject begins to move out of view of the window the tripod and camera will have to be dragged to another or rear window. This is not conducive to shooting a good video of the subject.

Instead of doing that, have a tripod dolly made or buy one (See *Figure 9*). They're cheap and extremely effective, giving good, professional quality video. The better the video, the more assignments that will come your way.

> The best tripod to use, we feel, is the *Tiltall* brand. It does not have a floating ball head. Most camera buffs swear by floating ball heads. They are good, but they have one big drawback. They cannot be tilted to the left, mainly because of the way the ball system works. This drawback becomes especially important when you're parked and the street or surface you are filming from is not level. The camera buff's response to that is to say, "...adjust the legs." Do you know how much time is lost fooling around with getting the legs adjusted just right, especially when your subject appears and you are not ready? Frustrating.

Because you have a camcorder does not make you a photographer or an investigator. It just makes you another individual with a camcorder. What sets you apart is how you use your camcorder, how you configure it. When you do purchase a camcorder, do it with one thing in mind —

SURVEILLANCE

CAMCORDER SELECTION TIPS

AC/DC

When purchasing your camcorder (as we did ours) make sure it will have AC/DC capabilities. This way you can plug an additional $19.95 plastic battery adapter into your auxiliary battery system and run the thing for two straight days without re-charging. Some camcorders do not have AC/DC capabilities. Think this out before you buy. Consider all the alternatives.

LUX

Determine what the lux is on the camera you want. The lux is vaguely defined as the amount of low level light conditions under which the camcorder will record. Our camera is a 3 lux. For a long time the best we could expect from a camcorder was 7 lux, early evening came and we couldn't film due to lack of light. Then came camcorders with an override switch that would bring them from 7 lux to 1 lux. An example is the Panasonic PV330. With the 1 lux capability, however, we noted a *strobe effect* when recording, which makes it look like someone was tampering with the video tape. The 7-to-1 camera went by the wayside...

HEAT, COLD and HUMIDITY

The only real problem we have experienced with our camcorders is excess heat and cold, and sometimes humidity. When the temperature reaches the high nineties outside the van it is over 110 inside. When the outside temperature approaches the 100 degree mark, inside it will reach 120. At this point the camera will shut down, and indication it's getting pretty hot in the van.

Conversely, if the temperature drops below 32 degrees inside, the camera will shut down. If the humidity is too high, the camera will detect there is too much liquid in the air and as a precautionary measure shut down while indicating "dew" in the viewfinder.

PHOTO EQUIPMENT

You've just filmed your subject after following him to work. You feel good about the shoot, however you never got closer than 100 yards.

You take the film to your client, proud of the video you have just completed. You play the tape on their VCR. The client doesn't say anything until it's halfway over. The client the casually says, "When will the subject appear?" You respond, *"You mean that's not the subject we've been watching all this time?"* "No, it's not, I have no idea who that is."

It's now time to learn about the next piece of equipment that is necessary for surveillance — a 35mm auto-film advance, auto-film rewind camera. In our company, we use Minolta Maxxum 7000 cameras with data backs. This camera is capable of being loaded, taking 12 photos in rapid succession, and being rewound and unloaded in 60 seconds. We use Kodak ASA 400 with 12 exposures. That's *color* film, by the way.

This camera body will cost about $270.00 on the average. With this flexible a body design, we use the normal 50mm lens, a 35-70 mm lens, and 80-200mm lens, a Soligor 500mm fixed mirror lens, and a Celestron C-90 spotting scope mirror lens. A doubler will fit all of the above lenses, giving them twice their normal focal length capability. Had the C-90 been on a tripod right next to the camcorder we could have taken what we call I.D. shots. That C-90 (which is 1000mm) will take the pictures of a subject at unbelievable ranges. Hand in good photos with the video tape and there will be no mistake as to who the subject is. If he denies that that is in him in the video tape, if he does, just produce the photos. End of case.

Figure 9. Some of the interchangeable lenses used on Cobra's Milolta Maxxum 7000.

Figure 10. Minolta Maxxum 7000, showing Data Back for Time/Date Verification.

We have two Maxxum 7000s in my van. One is continuously connected to the C-90 (*See Figure 11*) and the other is used for taking I.D. shots a closer ranges. I switch the 80-200mm lens to the 500mm lens and so on. The data bank imprints the date or time in the corner of the photograph. (*See Figure 9*).

Figure 11. Tripod-Mounted Maxxum 7000, mounted with C-90 spotting scope lens.

Develop the film ourselves? Not a chance. Any one-hour photo is worth $4-5 dollars. Your time is too valuable. We use only color film as black and white is just that, black and white. If the subject says (and with good reason) "that's not me," when viewing a video shot from a great distance, he may get away with it, unless:

> You've filmed him on the roof laying shingles wearing a red checkered shirt, blue jeans, tennis shoes and a red baseball hat; and, you also took some photos.

> If they were in black and white, all you will see is black and white. He might walk, if he's not clearly identifiable in the remotely shot video.

> If you took my advice and used the color film, the camera brought in his face, red checkered shirt, blue jeans, tennis shoes and a RED ball cap. No mistake. You've just nailed him, and destroyed his credibility in front of the judge.

That's what your job is all about. Creating evidence so strong there is no margin for error. Sometimes, a camera photo is ALL the evidence you can provide your client concerning a subject's activities. Be absolutely certain your photos totally support any claims about the subject your report may make, because you may have to *support* your *report* in *court*.

HIS WORD WAS GOOD ENOUGH?

> An investigator was assigned a case from a client. He was a smooth young man, with what he thought was a gift of gab. He knew how to get the cases, however he was not properly trained to conduct surveillance.

> He too cases anyway and, as one might expect, did not fare as well as he could have. He began turning in huge bills and strange evidence. This strange evidence was interesting to say the least. The insurance adjustor told me to look at this, so I looked at a picture of a house out in the country. Perplexed, I said, "Yes, this is a house in the country. Now what?"

> "Well another investigator took this picture and expects me to us it in court

with his testimony." I still wasn't sure what he was getting at, and then he said, "This investigator's report said, 'The subject was just behind the house, just a digging' away and plantin' a garden,' and the reason he knows is he saw him do it; however, there was no place the investigator could set up to document this on film, and he felt his testimony in court would suffice." Needless to say it was one (supposedly injured) claimant's word against the word of one paid-for-hire investigator with no documentation except a picture of the subject's house.

"*Right there, Your Honor, right there he was just a diggin' away.*" Pointing at the picture, opposing counsel asked if the young P.I. had any proof of these accusations. He (the investigator on the stand) said, "*Well, I saw him!*" "No that won't do," the counsel said as he brought in the claimant's younger brother, who closely resembled the claimant and asked, "Isn't it possible this is the man you may have seen in the garden?" "*Well...I was sure it was the right man.*"

To make a long story short, had this investigator taken a recognizable photo of the subject, this all could have been prevented. His credibility was injured and his case load began to drop. Remember,

LET YOUR EVIDENCE DO THE TALKING!

Assuming you have the proper training, all you need is the proper equipment. As you've seen, that's part of what this book is about — acquainting you with where to get the proper equipment.

You can get the C-90 at any good camera shop, used, for around $250.00. New it will cost anywhere from $400.00 at a discounter to $800.00 at a typical retailer. Look in magazines such as *Modern* or *Popular Photography*. You'll find scads of ads displaying this equipment. Don't worry whether or not it will fit your camera as adapters can be bought locally for as little as $9.00 to $20.00. The rest of your lenses can be purchased just about anywhere, new or used. Some of my equipment came from pawn shops, some came from classified ads in the newspaper and some was purchased at full retail right over the counter in good camera shops. If you cut corners it will show in your work. If you're not careful, buying cheap is buying twice.

Now, you will need a second Tiltall tripod for your C-90. Position it right next to your camcorder and while your camcorder is recording snap a few photographs (see *Figure 14*). Cover yourself. Even if you only take two photos and develop only two photos it will be worth the cost of processing a roll when it gets to court. Don't wait until you shoot the entire roll, get it developed immediately. Of course, you'll need another Tiltall tripod and another tripod dolly.

All the rest of your lenses on your back-up camera can be hand held and with practice you'll be taking photos like a pro. With these cameras, your only concern is a good clear photo.

Figure 12. Minolta Camera mounted on Tiltall tripod, next to camcorder.

My partner has the Canon line of camera equipment. She has a Canon T-90. The body of that camera costs $475.00. It too has auto film advance, auto-film rewind. This camera is capable of taking 5 1/2 photos per second. In other words, she can use up a whole roll of film of 12 exposures in 2 3/4 seconds. Taking more I.D. shots than that is a waste. Photos are only for identification. They do not show a range of motion or movement, like video show. *Back up your video with good photos.*

Sandi's camera also has a data back and the same lenses I have on my Minolta. She also has two tripods and her own van with the same equipment. I know camera buffs cringe at the thought of not setting the F-stop manually or shutter speed manually for the proper lighting etc. We are investigators, not photographers. I don't have time to adjust all that. All I want to do is aim and shoot. We get good clear photographs, identifiable photographs and the client doesn't care whether or not the photos will win some fancy contest.

Do not get a manual camera. Not only is a manual camera almost impossible to use in a quick-response surveillance situation, but eventually you'll be upgrading your equipment and the manual camera you bought last year won't be worth a nickel. If you don't believe me, go into a pawn shop and look at all the used cameras. They are 99% manual and you might find an Canon T-50 for $175 @ 1 1/2 frames per second. No auto rewind. *Buying cheap is buying twice, remember?*

Let's review what we now have in our arsenal with which to do surveillance:

- ❑   We have one camcorder with one two-hour battery (that comes with the camera);

- ❑   one auxiliary plastic AC/DC car cord battery for long term camcorder use;

- ❑   two auto film, auto rewind cameras with an array of adaptable lenses;

- ❑   two tripods, two dollies for the same and we're set, right?

Well, let's say your C-90 is set up out the back window of your van, while on station near your subject's home. You hear some noises, you look out the front of your van, and lo and behold! Your subject, his wife, and kids are out taking a leisurely stroll. It will be too cumbersome to grab your C-90 so it would be nice to have a good pair of binoculars handy just for purposes of identification.

BINOCULARS

A pair of 10 x 50 binoculars is awfully strong and would be hard to hold on a particular subject. While it does reach out there and see what you want to see, we recommend 8 x 40 power (*See Figure 16*). It combines clarity and stability in a far more balanced way than does the 10 x 50. Using binoculars is a lot easier than grabbing a camera just to see who is out there.

> *METHOD: When moving around in a parked surveillance van, careful, quite movements are necessary, so that you don't spook your subject, or passersby.*

You continue your surveillance. Your subject appears and you begin filming. His entire family exits the property and they all head for the family car. Do you pursue and possibly compromise your position? Or do you stay put?

Our experience says that in the early stages of the investigation, stay put. You are now getting down a pattern with this individual. You wait until he returns home, taking good, clear, generic, *brief* notes.

> *METHOD: Do not color your note taking with descriptive adjectives. Just the facts. Even then, be brief. The more detailed information you put into a report, the worse off you'll be when you get into court. It will give the opposing counsel more of an opportunity to pick away at details when trying desperately to discredit you. More on this later.*

The subject comes home in a couple of hours, and you make note of this. After he's home for 15 minutes he takes off again. Do not follow. He's gone 30 minutes and this time returns with a large sack of groceries. Apparently these were items the family missed when they went to the store the first time.

Thirty minutes later he comes out again, this time he leaves in a different vehicle and is gone one hour. *Do not pursue*. Repeat. *Do not Pursue*. With all the above information it should be clear to you, the subject is active, moves about quite a bit, but everything you've accomplished will be blown if you move, because you don't yet have compromising video of your subject's activity.

Now's the time to bring in a second investigator. You've seen which direction the subject leaves, so place the investigator several blocks away in his van. More on this later.

CHAPTER 6: Communications

This brings us to our next piece of equipment. A radio. It doesn't have to be expensive (although we have several that are, which we will tell you about shortly).

THE GOOD OL' BOY
If necessary, you can start off with a CB radio. You can buy a CB, installed, with a three way (AM/FM/CB) antenna for less than $150.00 total.

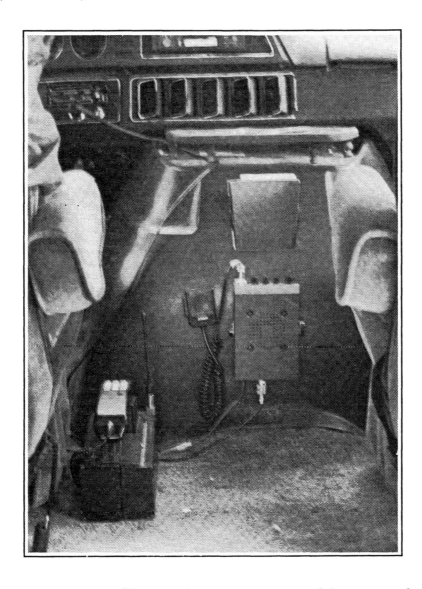

Figure 13. The Basic Radio — a CB mounted on the engine cover of the van; out of public view, but accessible.

This radio will be the best investment you will have made when your subject decides to leave. Just radio to your helper/partner/backup that he's leaving and in what vehicle, with the plate number.

A brief written report might go something like this:

9:00 A.M. Set up surveillance.

9:20 A.M. Subject exits house, places garbage on the curb. (See video).

10:45 A.M. Subject leaves, second investigator spots subject pass his position and is now in pursuit. Subject is followed to a hardware store.

11:20 A.M. Subject exits store and returns home with small package. (See video)

12:30 P.M. Subject exits home and pours contents of package purchased earlier into lawn spreader. (See video)

2:00 P.M. Subject secures from yard, enters home.

4:30 P.M. No more movement, investigators secure for the day.

Now what really happens at 12:30 P.M. is that when the subject comes out (bad back and all) he bends over, pours fertilizer in the spreader, picks up the spreader, carries it to the other side of the yard and begins pushing it around the yard. Every now and then, he stops, picks up a few bricks and throws them off to the side.

He picks up a bike, carries it to the garage, continues fertilizing the yard, stops and decides there are too many paper cups and other trash strewn about the yard to continue, so he momentarily discontinues, and goes around the yard bending over and picking up the trash (something he told the doctor he couldn't do).

All of this, you **don't** put in your report. *Repeat, this is not to go into written* *form.*

First of all, although you suspect it may be fertilizer he's spreading, you can't actually read the bag, so don't say what you don't know and can only suspect. Don't even mention you suspect it. Let the video tape say everything. (*Do not speak while recording.*) If a picture is worth a thousand words, this will be a doozie. Despite any claims to the contrary, your subject will have one difficult time getting out of this one. As much as you would have liked to mention what he was doing, just put the notation (*See video*) in your report. That keeps you out of trouble, your credibility high, and your services in demand. More on this later.

Back to the Radio. Your first reaction to a CB radio is that everyone can get one. Yes they can, but they don't. If you do have interference from eavesdroppers, do as we do and develop a system that is exceptionally hard to break:

METHOD: Use four channels. Channels 8, 18, 28 and 38. Start off on channel 8. If you get some clowns listening to you or interfering with your work or if you just don't want them in on your conversation, tell your partner to go up one. Your listeners will laugh as they turn their radios to channel 9 to see if you are stupid enough to talk on the designated emergency channel. Not a chance. You've just gone to channel 18. One bank of ten channels. Go up two and you'll find yourself on channel 28, up three to 38. Slick. You can bounce all over the radio, and it will take people a while to break this code. By that time, your surveillance should be over and done (several days). You don't have to use channel 8: this is just a suggestion.

CB radios, using a three-way antenna, will give about a four mile range over residential terrain. With taller buildings around, figure about a two mile range.

Mount the radio on the engine cover. This way it will be concealed from the average passerby and when you are on surveillance all you need to do is reach under the curtain, down the volume and talk away. No one will be the wiser. The important factor is outside antennas (the lack thereof). The last thing you need to do is arrive in a neighborhood looking like a submarine that just floated to the top of the water. ***Do not use a CB antenna.***

THE TPX

A second radio we have implemented in our firm is the GE TPX hand-held (police style) radio. This radio operates similarly to cellular telephones. The radio has a range of 60+ miles in town (on Channel 1) and out of town has a range of about 5 miles on Channel two. By the way, the first channel with the longer range is a closed circuit system and which no one can monitor. It operates off a repeater station, thus giving the desired distance.

The second channel operates much like the CB. It has about a 4-5 mile range and is just as good as a CB. The drawback to this radio is that its batteries

Figure 14. 8x40 power binoculars; GE TPX hand-held radio; transportable cellular phone.

last about 8 hours with minimal use. With normal use, you get about 6 hours of use. The way to increase the duration is to buy additional batteries at $80.00 each. TPXs cost about $1,195.00. In exchange for the extra range and portability, we feel the cost is justified. If you are on surveillance by yourself and it is determined that a second or third investigator is needed, with this powerful radio in your arsenal, help could be on the way immediately, without having to break your cover.

After the initial outlay for the radios (which can be lease-purchased) the monthly service to operate these radios is $11.50 per month. Actually, cheap communications.

TRANSPORTABLE CELLULAR

Our third method of communication is with transportable cellular telephones (*See Figure 16*). The key word here is TRANSPORTABLE. We can take them with us anywhere. The phones have a 3-watt output, and standby time nearly 10 hours. Talk time is two hours (before the battery runs down). When originally purchased, these phones ran about $1,695.00. The cost is considerably less now.

There are several advantages to having a transportable phone in the van:

❑ Immediate access to your office answering machine. You are able to retrieve your messages via the mobile, while on surveillance, and even call back a client or two. I find this impresses some of my clients, when I tell them I am actually watching someone at the same moment I am talking to them.

❑ After you arrive at a surveillance location and you've been set up for about an hour, and no movement whatsoever is detected, you can call the subject on the mobile. If there's no answer, obviously they are not home. Depending on the time of day, you can decide to stay and wait for the subject to come home, or you can leave, saving you client money by spot checking later. One drawback to this decision is that you won't be able to develop a pattern without watching the home. So you may want to stay. The advantage to the client if you leave is you will be saving him money. However, in the long run it will take longer to develop a pattern of the subject's movements. Weigh them out and decide what's best in any given situation.

❑ Besides the cost of the unit, each call you make will cost as much as 40 cents depending on the area you are in.

❑ The antenna is attached to the unit and is about 5 inches high. Therefore there is no need for external antennas.

❑ The unit will also run off of AC/DC power. This unit can be plugged into your cigarette lighter. Nifty.

❑ Now the disadvantage: someone at home can also call you when you are in the middle of filming someone, to bring home a loaf of bread. Ouch. If that is caught on film there will be some giggles in the courthouse.

CHAPTER 7 Keeping Comfortable

IT'S ALWAYS TOO HOT (or Too Cold)

In all actuality, when the temperature inside the van (did I mention the need for a cheap thermometer?) reaches 120 degrees it would be wise to do one of two things:

☐   Cease what you are doing, as heat stroke will shortly follow or

☐   Make sure you have a cooler full of ice, plenty of water and something to empty your bladder in.

Also have yourself stripped down to the bare essentials in clothing. No shoes, socks, shirts or hats for men. For women, it would be best to bring a swim suit along with you. Believe me, this is serious stuff, trying to do surveillance and maintaining an even body temperature.

> In 1987, I suffered heat stroke on a double team surveillance and by 4 P.M. I radioed my partner that I was in trouble. She immediately took me to the hospital where it took 4 more hours to start feeling halfway normal. Needless to say, surveillance was over for this day.

In the winter a propane heater with a small parabolic dish attached ($20.00) keeps the van nice and toasty. Using propane though, one must remember that ventilation is necessary. Open a window for a short time, get some air, then go back to surveillance.

You might not learn about the things I have just mentioned, until you are out there on the street, suffering. Which may be too late.

> Since the greatest percentage of your surveillance may well be done from a van, we will speak in terms of doing our work in that manner. It is necessary to know that on some occasions it is impractical to try to video from a van. If it looks like you'll have to abandon the van to get the video, by all means do so. If the only way to get there is on foot, get a large pack, load your camera and necessary items and go. However the van is the

safest to do surveillance from.

Which reminds me, we've done surveillance on members of police department SWAT teams. If you don't think that was harrowing...!

The ULTIMATE Necessity

When you arrive in an area, quickly survey the area to find place to park. Then, when set up, all the basic necessities of life will become noticeable — *by their absence*, if you don't plan well. To illustrate:

> Picture yourself at 5:30 A.M. You're heading out your driveway to do surveillance, and halfway there, with your eyes only open part way, you desperately begin looking for a convenience store to get a cup or mug of coffee. Ah! You've found one.
>
> It' 6:00 A.M. You've set up your camera. It's mid-October and a tad cold outside. You are sitting in the middle of your van behind the driver's seat in your short-term surveillance chair. The cup of coffee, with steam still coming out the cover, is held between your knees.
>
> You are beginning to get a little uncomfortable as your bladder is beginning to fill up. Male or female when nature calls, it *calls*. This brings us to the next piece of equipment that is necessary for long term surveillance.
>
> A $69.00 porta-potti purchased at K-Mart will do the trick.
>
> **Another reason why a car is impractical for surveillance. I mean, can you imagine trying to use a porta-potti while conducting surveillance in a residential neighborhood from a CAR?**

Place your porta-potti in the wooden camera case structure designed to hold all your equipment (*see Figure 17*). Use as needed. It will be good for about fifty flushes. You many not think this is important now, but wait until you've been out there for three hours, and you are convinced your subject is not going anywhere:

As you begin to put away your equipment you notice movement at your subject's home. He comes out in a suit and places the garbage on the curb. You drag out your equipment again. Now you REALLY gotta go to the bathroom. You can't compromise your position. You know you are about to get your subject on film. It'll be just a little longer. About then is when you learn to appreciate your new bathroom. K-Mart, Wal-Mart, Sears, etc. all carry these items. Check them out.

Figure 15. Storage Cabinet keeps Porta-potti, cooler, etc. out of way but handy.

IMPORTANT CONVENIENCES

ColorVideo Monitor

Our next piece of equipment, which is not an absolute necessity, is a television monitor. My personal unit is a 9" color unit with a swivel base (see *Figure 18*), which operates off AC/DC power. I have the camcorder where I want it to be, have it zoomed at the proper distance and sit back in my long term surveillance chair, and wait. After filming or watching anything through your camcorder viewfinder (which is black and white) for any length of time, your eyes will go numb on you. Watching the color monitor is as different as riding a bicycle vs. riding a motorcycle. No effort. It was purchased for $269.00 complete. What a deal.

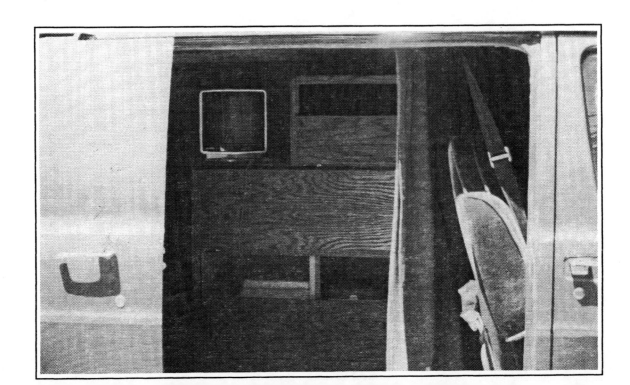

Surveillance Chairs

The long-term surveillance chair is a high-backed van seat that swivels and reclines at the flip of a lever. The chair is mounted on a box frame 2 inches high by 15 inches wide by 22 inches long. The long-term chair is soft and comfortable. While you watch your subject's home, you can be relaxing, if that's possible, while drinking fluids.

When things begin to happen, a quick move to the short-term surveillance chair is made. This chair is made out of wood and the back is about 18 inches high; the seat is about 10 inches off the floor and the seat itself is about 9 inches x 9 inches. It's sturdy and designed to keep you off your knees while filming. Rug burns will set in if you don't use it.

At first glance, the chair looks like it ought to be in a kindergarten class somewhere. Possibly, stolen from the same. But it's not, and it's an extremely valuable tool.

A Large Cooler

The next piece of equipment is an Oscar cooler by Coleman (See *Figure 17*). It's about 15 inches high, 10 inches across and 15 inches wide. Fill it with a bag of ice, a glass jug of water and you are on your way. If you plan on staying out all day, take a sandwich or two, maybe some potato chips. ***Do not take sodas.***

Repeat, do not take any carbonated sodas. Coke, Pepsi, Dr. Pepper or any other soft drink will dehydrate you and accelerate dizziness, nausea, light headedness and sleepiness. Drink only water. It cannot be emphasized enough to drink water. Gatorade is about the only drink other than water you may want to take, as it does have the proper nutrients to replace the fluids you have lost during the surveillance.

Long-term Surveillance is in Excess of Six Hours.

With this amount of time facing you, comfort will be extremely important. Watching someone's home from 5:30 A.M. till dark can emotionally and physically drain you. You may wait eleven hours before you even see your subject, and then it may only be for 3 minutes. However, those three minutes, with the proper attorney, can turn into a lifetime when presented in the court room. I have seen it done:

The claimant sits and squirms just after saying, under oath and under the threat of perjury, that his knee hurts so bad he needs help to walk to the car? The video shows that no only did he go to the car unaided, he stood and exchanged pleasantries with the neighbor for three minutes! His eyes will roll, he'll get angry (usually, not at you but himself, for being so stupid.) and say something like, "HE WAS INVADING MY PRIVACY."

Once you've acquired the practical basics in the way of long-term surveillance equipment, the rest is up to you. Experience will determine what items to add or subtract from your arsenal of necessary and optional gear. For example, a small $5.95 fan may work fine for you, while in some areas it just wouldn't be adequate.

CHAPTER 8: Security

Picture yourself in a van, in the middle of a residential neighborhood, camera at the ready, sweat running down your face and you're waiting for your subject to appear.

> It is summer and your rear windows are open, curtain, cracked 2-3 inches, enough to have the camcorder lens able to peer out. The front windows of your van are down, and you're ready. *Expect the unexpected.* You hear noises from outside, very near the van. It's teenagers talking about (and doing) the things teenagers talk about and do. *Pay attention.* A new problem has cropped up.

SECURITY

Teens are curious about everything, and if your windows are down, be prepared to handle the situation if they decide to reach in or worse yet open the door. No, there are no simple answers on how to handle this, however, here is just a small sample of what could happen:

> Recently a two investigator team I was involved with set up surveillance behind a strip mall. We were in the alley with a good view of an apartment complex only 50 yards away. After we were in place about half and hour, two young males around 22 years old cruised by the van and stopped their car. The driver said to the other passenger, "Na, there's no one in there." They circled the alley and were gone. I sat back down after they were out of sight. Several minutes later I heard this noise coming from the passenger side of the van. I looked around the main curtain and saw this arm opening the door. As he reached in, I grabbed my 9mm, uttered a few profanities, and took up the chase.

> In the meantime, our subject had come out and watched me pursue this individual (she didn't know where I came from). I chased the attempted thief around the corner of the building, where the same vehicle we saw earlier was parked, and this young man jumped in. I was about 50 yards away and yelled, "Freeze." I took a pistol stance, aimed, and yelled "Freeze," again. They both ducked, hit the gas, and drove off like I actually

was going to shoot. I got their plate, but it was registered to a Toyota and their car was a Pontiac Sunbird. Oh well.

I walked back to the van and the subject was still puttering around, moving things from her car to her apt. She finally left, drove about 50 yards and stopped. Sat there for several minutes and then returned to the apartment.

About 15 minutes later, she re-appeared, only this time with a two year old child in her arms. She was going to leave this kid at home while she went to go to therapy. Child abuse, neglect on film. The things that happen while on surveillance. Don't put anything past anyone, for any reason.

CHAPTER 9: Are You a Surveillance "Player," or Are You Just Playing Games?

Another reason for writing this book is to weed out the serious *surveillance* investigator from the *general* investigator. The general investigator has a 35mm camera, a pair of binoculars, maybe even an 80-200 mm lens, and he is convinced he can do surveillance (in his Volkswagen). I mean, after all, what is there to surveillance that is so difficult? Put that same investigator in a van for six hours straight and see how he feels. *If you have a full bladder, if you have a stiff neck or back or if you miss your subject, it's because you are not using the proper equipment; and, you don't have the proper training.*

SMOKING and "SERIOUS SURVEILLANCE"

This is a short story and won't take long, but it illustrates an important point.

About a year ago, all our investigators were totally overloaded with business, swamped. Calls were still coming in to do cases. I called upon another investigator, who after seeing our setup, convinced himself he too should get a van. After seeing him drive up in a properly "neutralized" van, I assumed he was committed to quality surveillance work. I subcontracted out to him and gave him an assignment.

Later in the day, I went to check on him and tried to raise him on the radio. Wasn't able to get him. Upon arriving, I parked about 4 car lengths behind him and wondered what to do to get his attention, just to let him know I was around if he needed me. After sitting several minutes, watching him, (not spying, just watching) I began noticing something very unusual. There was smoke coming from the side window of the van. I thought I was seeing things, so I got in the back of my van, looked through by binoculars and saw another small cloud of what appeared to be smoke come out. Every couple of minutes this puff of smoke was coming out of the van. No longer did I need my glasses. I could now see it with my naked eyes.

HE WAS SMOKING!

I guess I don't know many investigators who don't smoke. If you do, I would not recommend doing surveillance. Puffs of smoke tend to give away one's presence. On second thought, if you are an investigator, and you smoke, now would be a good time to stop. It'll be good for business and better yet, your health.

FOLLOWING UP SOMEONE ELSE'S SLOPPY SURVEILLANCE

Over the years, I have had many an occasion visit with other investigators and ask their views on surveillance. In particular, I remember one guy who was very adamant about not spending more than 2-3 hours on a case if he saw nothing. Later that night I found out why.

> He parks 3-4 blocks away, smokes his cigarettes, sits in his Chevy Blazer, and runs his air conditioner! Waiting, on the off-chance the subject will accidentally wander his way. He scoffed at the idea of doing long-term surveillance. Now I know why. He doesn't have the equipment and was not about to go out and buy it. Didn't think it was necessary. I don't think he's in business anymore.

If there is anything you should shy away from, it is a client who has already hired the Egotistical Private Eye (who's botched up the case) and who wants you to make things right. The problem is, your subject will already be on his guard because he's already spotted the idiot who was responsible for your being called in on the job. Trying to catch this subject will be next to impossible.

> *But, if you do take case, make darn sure you do what you're hired to do. Because if you succeed, you will be a hero and the cases will roll in. Of course, if you take the case and fail, then you'll have confirmed the client's low opinion of P.I. surveillance, injuring chances of repeat business for your firm, and the image of the reputable surveillance P.I. in general.*

SOMETIMES, A POLICE BACKGROUND HELPS...

Another interesting thing I have noticed is that most investigators have police background. *This is fine if you've also had detective training.* Most policeman do not get in-depth detective training.

In our city, while going through the academy, *cadets must go through 200 hours of surveillance in a van.* A life sentence for most, but many city don't even require that much. At the age of 45, I have logged over 25,000 hours of surveillance since 1965.

Most investigators do not care for surveillance. They consider it too boring. Most want to do those Mike Shayne-type criminal cases. If that's you, you might think this book is not for you. However, a little research on your part will show that the majority of the work (and the money!) is in surveillance. Does that little tidbit of information change your attitude?

CHAPTER 10:   Teaming

After a few surveillance jobs, you're going to start wishing for a CLONE of your properly equipped surveillance van standing by:

> Your subject begins to move; you decide to pursue. You quickly secure your equipment and take off in the van.

> Besides other drivers on the road, you will discover old frustrations, like:

> ❑   stop lights

> ❑   people parked at stop lights

> ❑   people blocking both lanes of traffic leaving you unable to pass

> ❑   police officers

> ❑   orange barrels directing traffic from three lanes into one lane where the traffic is backed up two miles

> ❑   School zones @ 15 mph.

> While in pursuit, any one (or all) of these things will confront you. Even if they don't or you are somehow able to circumvent them, you will probably find your subject going to a local grocery store — only to find he got a parking space right near the entrance; *and the only other spot to park is 16 spaces away, with a pickup truck with a camper shell on it in your way.*

If a second surveillance vehicle is employed, you'll be more comfortable with the knowledge that you have doubled your chances of securing a good video.

Normally, one vehicle is used where the subject can be seen coming and going. If the subject is one of those who does a lot of moving around, filming at his residence won't be necessary, but following him will be. A couple of pointers to keep in mind when following:

1. Stay in the right lane most of the time. If this is not possible, the center lane is best; this way you can respond to either a right turn or left turn at the last moment.

2. When approaching an intersection, while keeping your subject about 3/4 of a block ahead of you, speed up while going through. However when through the intersection slow down to let the subject get some distance from you.

3. If you are using only one pursuit vehicle, and you see that the subject is going through a yellow light, and it turns red before you can cross, you have two choices:

    ❏   You blow off the pursuit and hope for better luck next time.

    ❏   If you believe that continuing the pursuit is important enough, you stop at the intersection, (we do not promote, or approve of the following) then blast of right through it, **first making sure it is clear in both directions.** *The last thing we want to do is create down time for our vehicles, or injuries to others.*

    We have sometimes had to activate the second option, and have never been caught, yet this is not to say that it is not wrong to do. We occasionally have to do it when we can't work with a second, team vehicle, but that doesn't make it right.

TEAM PURSUIT

A second investigator traveling in front of your subject can be exceptionally useful, assuming of course you know where the subject is going. *Have you ever been followed by someone when they were in front of you?* With radios, it's possible.

The techniques are fairly simple, provided your leading van is equipped similarly to the trailing van. The lead unit stays fairly close to the subject, no more than 3 or 4 cars in front. That way, if the trailing unit sees the subject signal for a turn, he can radio the lead unit in time for the lead unit to make the same turn ahead of the subject. Two units working together can even track a very suspicious subject by playing the surveillance game of *Leapfrog*...

❑   If the trailing unit gets cut off by a missed light or some other obstacle, he can radio the lead unit to drop back and behind the subject. The cut-off unit can then, by following the instructions radioed by the still in-contact unit, cut through side routes and place himself in front of the subject a few blocks down the road.

❑   A variant of this technique is to periodically have the lead and trailing units swap places, while in the process of following the subject. First, the leading unit (who has been in front of the subject) drops back to a point behind the subject and just in front of what has been the trailing unit. Then the trailing unit speeds up and places himself in front of the subject. Since the same vehicles aren't maintaining fixed positions behind or in front of him all the time, the subject will be less likely to get suspicious.

METHOD: Find or hire a second investigator with the same equipment as you, same training or nearly the same training as you and you'll make a dynamite double team.

There are other instances where two vans become especially useful. Here's an example:

On one occasion, there was absolutely no place to do surveillance without looking out of place. We took our second van and parked it where we had the best vantage point and abandoned it. We made sure the curtains were open and it could be seen through at a distance. After 4 days of the new van sitting there it was no longer a visitor to the area.

In the early morning hours we slipped into the vehicle and the things we got on video convinced us our methods were right on the money.

CHAPTER 11: Creativity

What makes a so-so investigator a *good* investigator? Basically, his *creativity*. His equipment helps, but a robot can be taught to take pictures. It's the person doing the work that will get the credit. Being able to adapt one's self to the details of the specific job, the environment, the terrain — even the ethnic area leads to a good result from an investigation. The case must be studied, along with the area. Careful, thorough consideration of every detail is a must. Nothing can be overlooked. Somehow, a way must be found to complete your task.

THE CASE OF THE DUMPED DUMP TRUCK...

Not all our cases involve surveillance, but techniques we've learned in surveillance can be used in most situations. Case in point:

> Not long ago, I was asked by an insurance company to look into an accident involving a dump truck on a mountain road. The dump truck was a 1970 model Ford worth about $3,000. It was going up a mountainous road and just about made it when the engine conked out, rolled back about 30 feet into an embankment and tipped over, creating a total loss.

> The adjuster smelled a rat. The insurance had been purchased around noon on a Friday, and according to the sheriff's report the accident happened on the next day (a Saturday) at about 1:30 P.M. No witnesses were to be found, so based on the sheriff's report, the insurance company paid out approximately $9,000.00 on the claim. The insured balked and said he told his insurance man it was worth $20,000.00 when he purchased the insurance. He called the insurance company and told them the same thing. This was the first red flag.

> ❏ An insured does not tell an insurance company what a vehicle is worth; a network of auto dealers nationwide searches its computer banks and tells the insurance company what the *average market* of the vehicle is.

> The insurance company called me and asked me to look into all the facts

behind the report.

I arrived in this resort town about 5:00 P.M. I ate dinner, read the file once more, drove around a while after getting the lay of the land and then determined who I was going to visit with first. My first stop, I decided, would be the State Police. Sometimes, in small towns, local police have a personal involvement with a subject under investigation. In the event of any trouble with the local police, the state police at least knew we were there on official business.

Our next stop was the sheriff's office. The deputy we wanted to speak to hadn't arrived yet. In order for all of us to know what was going on, I requested a copy of the report taken on the day of the accident. The clerk began looking around for it. She began looking in all the usual places, with no luck.

The deputy arrived at that time and we greeted him and told him that as soon as we found the police report we could discuss it more intelligently.

He was unusually friendly, perhaps a bit uneasy, as we were officially looking into the details of his report. Unable to locate the report, I called the insurance company (I had a copy of the insurance company's report in my pocket, but the sheriff's people didn't know that). The adjustor gave me the report number, which was found to be out of sequence with the reports for the last several months. The accident had occurred *in May* but the report was one that was to be used *in January* (5 months earlier), a sure sign of sloppy administration.

The deputy disappeared while we were visiting with the undersheriff, and several clerks. A minute or two later the deputy showed back up with the report in hand! How convenient! I carefully examined it and then I began asking him questions. My first question was, "Did you write this report?" He answered yes. I asked, "Did you actually write this report in your handwriting?" I don't know why I asked that, but it occurred to me that it might help later (and it did, because he *hadn't* written the final report, although he said that he had done so!).

We asked the deputy if he would accompany us to the location of the accident. There was no problem, and off we went, following the deputy in our vehicle.

On top of a hill on a nearby mountain, he stopped his patrol car and said, "This is the place." I saw where the gravel was dumped, saw where the truck had turned over and then, after looking around a bit, it occurred to me. Where was the truck going? So I asked the deputy, who placed his hand on his hips and looked up the mountain. "I guess over to that house they were building, or to that house over there on the right." I thanked the deputy and started to walk away when he asked me what kind of investigator I was. For lack of anything else to say, although in this case it was very appropriate, I said I was an insurance fraud investigator.

His eyes opened up and I could see he was concerned. The deputy left and I proceeded up the mountain. The contractor at the house under construction remembered the accident because the driver had come up the hill to tell him he lost his load and to call his boss. *The contractor remembered it being a Friday,* because the men were all talking about it being a payday, and where they were going to get a brew. "Yes," he said, "it was a Friday." But he couldn't remember the date.

On to the next house. The senior male was not home but the son remembered the accident, and also remembered his dad was mad because the truck blocked the road when he wanted to come down it, and he had to stay home the majority of the day. Since the father wasn't home, we decided to come back. Around 1:00 P.M. we returned and the father said he couldn't remember the day or date, but said he did see the truck coming up the hill (it was making so much noise), saw it roll back down and tip over. He said this happened about 9:00 A.M., because it was the time he regularly leaves town. We thanked him and left for town, to speak to the sheriff.

I laid all the facts out on the table and asked why the report was dated on Saturday instead of Friday. The Sheriff said he remembered the incident well, as the owner of the truck was insistent on getting a report right away.

So, he sent his deputy out to investigate the accident. The deputy was told to bring the report back to the sheriff the next day, so he could check it over for legibility and any errors, knowing it would be read by an insurance company.

The sheriff got the report the following morning and began rewriting it. When he got to the date, he looked at his watch and put down Saturday's date, thinking, "What's the big deal?" The owner of the truck had said the accident occurred at 1:30 P.M. and with no witnesses, and no one injured, precision probably wasn't that important.

Thinking everything was in order, he gave a copy of the report to the owner of the truck. Needless to say, the "victim" was elated that the report date read Saturday as he had purchased his insurance on Friday at Noon, *2 1/2 hours after the accident occurred.* This made his claim look even better, knowing the police report corroborated his own misstatements.

The sheriff, being a tad concerned by my questions, checked the deputy's daily log and found that he had been dispatched to the area of the accident *on Friday* to take a report. This verified the accident did NOT take place on Saturday. Since the incorrect date on the report was due to an understandable mistake on the part of the Sheriff, no intentional fraud existed — on the part of the Sheriff's Office.

After getting all the information I could from all sources, it was determined that:

❑   the accident occurred at 9:00 A.M. as the witness said

❑   the owner ran to the site to see the damage, left for town and went right to his insurance agent and took out a policy on this wrecked bucket of bolts.

Which, of course, was *Not Nice.*

We left town. The next day, the sheriff visited the owner of the dump truck and ask him where the truck was. He told him it was in the back lot, that they didn't use it anymore. The sheriff told the man that some investigators had been poking around, asking questions. The man looked concerned and said he knew about it already. The sheriff went on to say that "...there was a witness who said the accident occurred at 9:00 A.M.; you said it happened at 1:30 P.M. Why did you lie to me?" The subject's reply was brief: "I still have the check the insurance company gave me; should I give it back?" The sheriff's answer was equally brief: "To keep yourself out of jail, that would probably be a good idea."

The check for $9,000.00 was returned and no criminal charges were filed. The subject had held the check for about two months. It was almost as if he suspected someone would find out. And we did. It took careful planning, careful questions and the fact that a P.I. was there looking into the case, which got EVERYONE a bit nervous.

Even though this case did not involve any conventional surveillance, it illustrates one of our Methods:

❑   it is important to get all the facts,

❑   keep your mouth shut,

❑   and listen.

❑   You always learn more by listening, and *learning is our business.*

In surveillance, we would say, "Get all the facts. The way to obtain those facts are on video tape. The video will tell the whole story, just keep your mouth shut..."

TIP: Get Video of the Surrounding Area for Confirmation:

❑ **To further "lock-in" the placement of an incriminating video, when in the parking lot of a grocery store, pan by the store name and maybe a street sign.**

❑ **The video should have the time and date on it.**

CLEAN VIDEOS FRUSTRATE OPPOSING COUNCIL

In Court, if your video is clean, thorough and quiet, opposing counsel won't have much to ask you and if he does, it will be to try to intimidate you. What can he ask? *What is your education?* Even if you had none (which is unlikely) so what? *The video speaks for itself.* He may ask how long you have been licensed, or how long have you been an investigator, or where you live (*by the way, he doesn't need to know that*). Don't panic! An attorney may only ask things relevant to the court hearing.

> One attorney, about April of 1987, asked one of my junior investigators all the usual, intimidating questions and was getting nowhere fast and it could be seen on his face.
>
> The more time went on, the more frustrated he became. He finally became so furious that without realizing what he was saying he blurted out. "WELL...WHAT COLOR WAS YOUR CAMERA?! " Defense counsel stood up and stated, "I object, Your Honor." The judge asked, "What relevancy does that have to this case counsel?" The shame-faced attorney replied, "Sorry, Your Honor, strike that question, please."

You never know what will happen in court, but rest easy. Answer all the questions with either a "yes" or "no" unless he specifies that you go into detail. If that happens keep your detail generic.

"TRIPLE-TEAMING" WORKS, TOO

There are a lot of cases where the subject becomes suspicious, or is tipped-off about an ongoing investigation. Sometimes, we'll use two investigators in one van. One investigator is in the back of the van, the other is acting as "camouflage" — working outside the van on a "break down."

At the same time we'll have a second van, with the investigator, on standby. The suspicious subject is put off his guard by his awareness of the "out-front" van, and relaxed enough for the second investigator to capture video from a different location. The opposing attorney may ask, "How did you know what my client was doing behind the house if you were watching from the front, and more importantly, how did you get this film?"

Your answer to that would be, "I had another investigator in the back of the van and we radioed to a second surveillance vehicle to do a drive by. So in all, there were three of us at one time or another watching this man."

Even if you are the only investigator present in the courtroom, it is unlikely the attorney would call for the other members of your team. With this kind of evidence (good video) and your confident statements, the more witnesses against him the less he'll like it. More than likely, he'll dismiss you from the stand and be wishing you'd never testified. Oh well..........

CHAPTER 12:   Over-Creativity

NO DIRECT CONTACT!

> *Being creative as a P.I. is important, but sometimes you might be tempted to go overboard. Don't succumb to temptation. It can only lead to trouble, loss of business, possibly your P.I. license.*

There are several things you should know prior to doing any surveillance:

- ❑   If the subject you are doing surveillance on is represented by counsel.

- ❑   If he is, your best bet is to have no direct contact with the individual, whatsoever.

- ❑   If you don't know, you should find out. Not only is it your duty to find out, it is your *responsibility*, to your client and to the well-being of your own firm.

- ❑   If you are unable to find out, go on the assumption that the individual *is represented* and do not, *for any reason,* come into direct contact with the subject of your surveillance.

Although there is no real law that prevents you from coming in contact with the subject. If the subject is represented by counsel, then the insurance company & you as its agent must go through the attorney to contact the subject, and may not contact the subject directly. It is considered unethical to come into direct contact and most judges, as well as people in the industry, frown on it. It can spoil your employer's case, even if you shot the world's best video. Some judges may even impose some heavy fines, if improprieties are discovered.

"CAN I TAKE YOUR PICTURE FOR MY CLASS?"

> *This actually happened not too long ago.* Remember the young P.I. who took a photo of the subject's house, then figured his own testimony would

be enough to win the court.

This same investigator was hired (by the same company-I know what you're thinking, but what can I say?) and in order to save face and redeem himself, he was under pressure to get something on this new subject, no matter what. Well, upon setting up surveillance, (van and all) he began hearing loud noises coming from the rear of this residential home. Unable to film from any remote location, he decided to use the direct approach.

He exited his van, camcorder in arm, and walked to the individual's house. He walked around back and discovered the subject was cutting a good down sized tree with an axe. Quickly he came up with the following: ".Howdy, I heard the noise and decided this was perfect for my students?" The claimant agreed and there he was: Filming away, on the subject's property, *under false pretenses.*

Ouch! As desperation sets in, investigators with otherwise normal heads do strange things.

RECORD WHAT YOU SEE!

The intelligent investigator realizes that when he is hired to look into anyone's activities, he is not there to "*get something*" on someone. He is there to do what he was asked to do — record their activities. Do not rope them into doing things they would not normally do, just *record their activities.* If they are not doing anything, record that. If they are walking with a cane, record that. WHENEVER you see the individual (with one exception) record the event.

THE EXCEPTION

The claimant goes to the doctor. He's there for an exam. You have been told you can identify him then and take a photo at that point. The over-zealous investigator, bound and determined to get this guy on film, sneaks over to his vehicle, *lets the air out of his tire,* gets back into his van, and waits. The . subject comes out and the investigator feels, "I've got him now!" He films him changing his tire. **DON'T DO IT!**

❑   One, it's one of the oldest tricks in the book. It's been done so
       often, it's almost always considered inadmissible as evidence, even if
       the flat tire is for real!

❑   Two, you are going to get blamed for setting up old "flat-tire-in-the-
       parking-lot" routine.

Even if you notice he has a perfectly legitimate flat tire while parked, *turn
that video camera away*. Document it by notes but do not mention it in your
report, or take a video. One more time: *you more than likely will be
blamed for his tire being flattened.*

NECESSITY OF LIFE

On the other hand, say you follow him home, and he has a blow-out a block
from his house. Stop and film this. This would be perfectly legitimate. You,
obviously, could not have caused this. However, even though this, more
than likely, would be acceptable video, there are a couple of arguments
your client's attorney and the subject's attorney could use in court which
would lessen the effect of the video:

Your Client's Attorney: "...if hurt so bad why didn't he call someone to help
with it?"

Claimant's Attorney: "...there was no one to call, so he fixed it himself."

This falls under the category of *"necessity of life."* This is something,
regardless of his medical condition, that he had to do. Change his tire. The
courts will usually allow this.

Changing the "Necessity of Life" Scenario a Bit:

You have a female subject with a 10 lb. lifting restriction. You set up
surveillance on her. She drives to the grocery store and buys 8 plastic
bags of groceries. You beat her home and set up across the street.

❑ The plastic bags have a 40 lb. burst rate with an average load of 22.5 lbs. This obviously is over the limit she can carry.

❑ *The law provides an exclusion in that the woman must eat.* Therefore, when she gets home she is allowed to carry one bag at a time in (even though it exceeds her restrictions). She must make 8 trips to stay within the necessity of life rule.

❑ *The minute she grabs more than one bag, one in each hand for example, or more out goes the necessity of life rule.* She would really be hurting and aggravating her own situation by carrying more than one bag. Therefore one would tend to believe she may be exaggerating her claim a tad.

ROPE-A-DOPE?

Another interesting "over-creative" surveillance technique is roping someone into doing something they normally would not do. One tale comes to mind when I used this investigator to follow this man.

> Over several days she was not able to come up with anything. She knew he was active, but her timing was off. One day in the course of this investigation, she heard from her rehab assistant of the rumor that the subject was cutting and delivering firewood on the side. A day or so later she came in with film of him unloading a whole cord of firewood (with a "bad back") and stacking it very nicely for the customer.

> I asked her how she was able to time it from beginning to end. She said it was easy. *"I called him up, ordered a cord of firewood for my mom, and he delivered it and was paid for it."* Off he went, a happy camper and off my investigator went, felling she had gotten what she needed.

> In the meantime, I'm sitting at my desk trying to figure a way out of this one. Needless to say, I kept my mouth shut for a couple of months, not knowing exactly what to do with this "new" evidence.

Eventually, the way the film was taken came up and the attorney who reviewed the tape discussed it with the investigator. I was not present. *Although she had heard rumor to the effect that he was cutting firewood, she saw no proof, until she lured him to do it.* The attorney wasn't too upset, just a little concerned.

He called me to his office to discuss the matter and indicated that the film would be useful *if* and *only if* the subject was advertising publicly that he was selling firewood. "In other words, Bob, go out to where he lives, scan laundromats, drug stores, community centers or wherever there are boards with consumers and citizens advertising for various things, and get me some evidence!"

Happy to say, the subject had advertised for the sale and delivery of firewood and I took the postcard down and rushed it back to the attorney. The investigator who took the film never really knew the subject was doing this stuff until she tricked him into actually delivering it. Now that we had his card advertising he did this, our collective tails were covered. A stern reprimand was in order. However, it could have been worse, had that evidence not been found.

☐ **Remember, if a subject advertises an activity he is not supposed to be performing to the general public, he is fair game. Film away!**

CHAPTER 13:   How Cobra Does It

Recently, my partner and I, working as a double team, had been working this female subject for several days. She was in an auto accident in 1986. Our investigation was in July 1990. She still "has neck and back pains, dreams of the accident all the time, can stand only 30 minutes before everything from the waist on down goes numb." She can drive for only thirty minutes at a time, then has to stop to get out to stretch. Sound familiar?

The job hadn't started out very positively. The attorney who called me stated we were "strongly" recommended by the insurance company, which had used us before and was pleased with our work. Begrudgingly, she called and assigned us the case. She also politely told me surveillance had never worked in the past for her, so, why were we any different?

"Hmm....," I thought to myself, "take her to your van and show her that you not only have the knowledge, you have the equipment." This is the first time I had ever shown my equipment to someone who acted as if they were seeing a Bic pen. This, needless to say, didn't leave me with a very positive an attitude.

Then, as we began working the case, it became harder and harder. I was sure we weren't even going to locate this woman. My partner persevered (Always does. I wouldn't have it any other way).

It turned out she lived with her parents. When people do this, rarely is there anything in their name that can be immediately traced. Especially in a two or three day surveillance. We used all the techniques, and still failed to a degree to find her as quickly as we normally would:

❑   we did the paper trail trip,

❑   checked all the utility companies

❑   cross reference directories,

❑   pretext phone calls.

❑   We even made a MONEY CALL. They hung up on us! First time!

Oh, well. We had been supplied the number; and we finally verified that it did go to the house we were told it did, but the subject's car was never around.

ONE MORE TIME: *Skip tracing is a basic fundamental for every investigator. Period. You must know skip tracing. After all you have to find your subject before you can do surveillance.*

SUGGESTION: Call Paladin Press. Their number is 303-443-7250. Ask for their catalog. I found several books on skip tracing and missing persons exceptionally well written; and in my opinion the authors definitely know what they are talking about. Read their catalog. They have a number of good books. You won't find these books in any mall or bookstore.

Getting on with the story...

One afternoon, after getting thoroughly frustrated with this lady, we happened on her quite by chance. With only one van, we set up surveillance about a block away. We set up our cameras and about 3:30 P.M. she came out. We were now convinced; she was alive; she did live where the adjustor told us she did and drove what the deposition said she drove.

She began to take off. We secured our equipment, jumped in the front of the van and took off after her. Even after running several stop signs and two red lights, we lost her. We were just not prepared to pursue with only one vehicle.

The next day we took two vans. One we parked 3 blocks ahead of her and the other in the same place as the day before. Sure enough, at 3:30 she came blazing out of her house and took off in the same direction. I immediately radioed my partner and she began what became a lengthy pursuit.

The woman headed in the general direction we expected her to go, so my partner was able to stay in front of her for about 4-5 miles, before she was finally overtaken by the subject.

I could not keep up with either vehicle and could only hope my partner could stay with the subject, who apparently was in a real hurry to get wherever she was going. She was up to 70 mph in a 45 mile zone. My partner radioed "she's switching lanes like Bobby Unser at the Indy 500." My partner, not to be outdone by this young whippersnapper, was keeping up, when all of a sudden the subject hit her brakes, banked hard left and turned into a parking lot where lumber supplies were sold.

By this time, I had caught up discovered the subject was not where my partner had said, but at the gas station next door where they had a food mart. The woman went in, got behind the cash register and away she went. From 4 p.m. until 1 a.m. she didn't sit down once, nor did her legs appear to give out.

At about 4:30, (a half-hour after our arrival), we made sure she wasn't going anywhere, and decided to come back after dark. About 9:00 p.m. we showed up and filmed her for two solid hours; bending down under the counter getting a sack for beer patrons bought, climbing up on the counter getting cigarettes, loading various groceries into brown paper sacks.

I finally decided to go in and see if she had a stool to sit on. I went in, purchased some gum, looked around as if I were trying to remember something (saw no stool) and went out to the telephone and made calls to my friends while leaving my van right out in front of the store. there were so many people coming and going, that the van sat in the same place for two hours while my partner shot two hours of video. It hasn't gone to court yet, but "...can't stand over thirty minutes..." Thbbbbbfff!

Note: even though we were filming the subject on private property, she was, legally, "in the public eye," so she was fair game. And good video.

In any event, we filmed our subject doing all the things she said she couldn't do, and another case will be coming in from the attorney who didn't believe this sort of thing was possible. *"Only in the movies do they get their man."* Not so. Specialize, and the cases will roll in.

ANOTHER NOTE OF WARNING: The techniques described in this book and the illustrations we use to make a point are for your entertainment only. Some of them are dangerous, others may be illegal where you live or work. Be cautious. If you decide, of your own volition, to attempt any of these techniques or procedures, at least practice them a lot before putting them into your repertoire. Please?

ON THE SIDE

I have been to several states where our Methods will not work. Hawaii, for example. There are no laws requiring homeowners to limit the size of their walls or fences around their homes. Vegetation grows around their homes like ragweed. If you can't even see the house, You'll have your work cut out for you. While vacationing there recently, I pictured myself doing surveillance there. I suppose it can be done, and in time I would be able to adapt as I am sure they have done there.

Maybe an investigator in Hawaii would wonder how to do surveillance here in the southwest. Speaking from experience and having done surveillance in Arizona, Colorado, Texas and New Mexico, there are laws in the southwest about how high a wall can be erected in front of your home, which makes it easier, in some cases to do remote surveillance.

Check your local codes prior to going outside your own area.

Of course, if you plan on doing surveillance in downtown Manhattan, a whole new set of rules will apply. Probably, a lot of it will be foot surveillance...

CHAPTER 14:   Privacy, Invasion Thereof

Invasion of privacy is one of the touchiest areas for the surveillance investigator. A good one will know what is invasion and what's not. Remember, however, this is an area where *you* can be sued. If you are not aware of this little law, I strongly recommend you look into it with an attorney and check case law.

In 1978, I believe, the Pennsylvania Supreme Court ruled in favor of an investigator who had filmed someone doing something he indicated he couldn't do. I feel it is your responsibility to know where to draw the line. Let me briefly touch on what we have been taught about invasion of privacy.

Anything that can be seen by a passerby can be filmed. There are laws from state to state about one- or two-party consent; however, in most states, the consent of only one party is necessary. Check with your lawyer. Since you are one of the two parties involved in the filming, you should be the one operating within the law. Here's a scenario:

> You drive by your subject's home to see him standing in the picture window in full view of God and everybody. He is fair game for picture taking.
>
> However, if he stands back about 8 feet in the same room and you find it necessary to make use of an aid that will enable you to film that far back into the shadows (say, an infra-red system) you are violating the individual's civil rights by invading his/her privacy. **DO NOT DO THIS.** It is not worth the penalties. We are not only talking city and state laws but mostly Federal laws. And the Feds usually don't mess around...

If you place yourself in a position that a passerby would not normally assume, in order to view and film your subject, you very well could have invaded his privacy. Do not do this. Think for yourself. Here's a test you can apply to your situation: *If I were a passerby, could I see this individual from my position?* If not, I would not recommend even trying to get film.

This also goes for trespassing. Unless you have express permission of the owner of the property you are on, even a public parking lot, it might be in your best (legal) interest to get permission. Of course, if you are good, you probably won't get caught. If you are trying to get good, and you get caught, you'll regret it. You'll wish you had asked before taking that video.

In court, opposing counsel will not normally ask you if you had permission or not unless the claimant wonders where in the devil you were since he did not see you. Then you may get asked under oath, how you obtained the damaging evidence. Better have a good story, like the truth, because it will come out.

In New Mexico where I reside, we have a rather unusual environment. We have a high (50.7) percent) Hispanic population. If you don't know how to pronounce various Spanish terms and names you will not fare well. Several Arizona P.I.s have moved their firms into New Mexico only to find this out for themselves. The Hispanic culture is totally different and must be learned. Consequently, they have had to hire N.M. investigators to supplement their own staff.

We also have block walls around our homes in lieu of wooden fences or no fences. In our backyards, most block walls are about 5 feet high. If your subject has a block wall one block higher than the surrounding neighbors, he is trying to maintain his privacy. If you can see him from another backyard without straining, that's ok. But if not, he is trying to preserve his privacy, which you may be invading. Do not climb on a roof, do not shimmy up a pole to film (unless you live in Manhattan). You will be violating his civil rights.

If there is any question in your mind, DON'T do it!

The methods we have mentioned work very well in our area. They may not work in your area. Adapt is the key word, wherever you are.

ONE MORE TIME

Don't use a car. This is a poor-man's way of doing surveillance. To be successful, you have to look and act successful and success will come your way. Really, use a van. Stay out longer than 2-3 hours and you will get your subject.

CHAPTER 15:   The Report

I'm going to elaborate a bit on something that I only touched on earlier about report writing. I recently finished reading a book about surveillance report writing. I was not comfortable with it and I'll tell you why.

His report:

❑   6:30 A.M.: I left my home to do surveillance on Mr. Jones.

❑   6:45 A.M.: I arrived to find two cars in the drive of a middle class neighborhood with a nice pink pitched roof home, with a white picket fence around the yard. It had two large bushes in front of the door which makes it hard to see the man coming out of his home. I moved several feet to get into position which was directly across the street in my Red Corvette. The cars in the drive had plate numbers JXY 198 and RDE 891, respectively.

❑   7:30 A.M.: I continued surveillance and finally saw a man about 40 with a hat on, long sleeves, what appeared to be blue jeans, about 6' tall, 200 pounds and a mustache exit the house, I began filming while he got into one of the two cars and drove away.

Our report: (in a van)

❑   6:30 A.M.: Left for subject's area to set up surveillance.

❑   6:45 A.M.: Upon arrival noticed two vehicles, one with plate number JXY 198 and the other RDE 891. No movement, continued surveillance.

❑   7:30 A.M.: Male meeting the description of the subject exits the home. (See video.)

Why the big difference in the report styles? Well, the first investigator feels the more information given on the report the more thorough an investigation he will have done.

While he's taking notes he's missing the curtains being opened and the front door being opened with the dog being let out. He feels the insurance company will love his detailed report, which shows how much effort was put into his investigation.

"Video? What Video? I had to write down the notes, besides he would have seen me in my car across the street." He turns in his bill, gets paid and goes his merry way. If it goes to court (expect them all to go to court, that way you'll be ready), you can imagine how the opposing counsel will have a field day with his report! What do you mean field day! Well...

On the stand, opposing counsel might say, "Your report is pretty thorough, Mr. Investigator. I was wondering, since you were so observant, did you see the subject limp, even a little to his car?"

A. Well...ah...I don't remember.

Q. What color hat was he wearing?

A. Well...ah...I don't remember that, either.

Q. Was it a baseball hat, fisherman's hat, cowboy hat or what?

A. Well, I know it wasn't a cowboy hat.

Q. It seems even though your report was thorough, you don't remember pertinent details, do you, Mr. Investigator?

With a Cobra-style report, counsel has nothing to pick at. You just wrote down generic facts. You didn't say where you were, which would give away the kind of vehicle you were in, you didn't give him any information.

> Most of the attorneys we do cases for never use reports in court, citing their tendency to get one into trouble. Most of our better attorneys don't even want a report. "Just give us a video, Bob. Do what you do best. The video will tell the story."

Who cares if he has two bushes in his front yard and how would you know what middle class is from other class? You are probably not an expert on this area, anyway. Don't try to be one now!

The only reason we create a report is to justify to our client the time we spent for billing purposes.

When we bring in a bill, a report, photos and a video tape what do you think the adjustor does? Look at the bill? Nope. Check out the pictures? Nope. *He grabs the video and heads for the conference room.* Your check will arrive in a couple of days. The stronger the video, it seems, the quicker the check. Worth thinking about...

Good hunting! Remember, practice makes perfect...

Cobra Company
"When no one else cares"

AUTHORIZATION FOR INVESTIGATIVE SERVICE

I _____, of the _____ Company hereby authorize Cobra Company to investigate the worker's compensation claim as listed below (if other than worker's comp., please specify.) In authorizing Cobra to do this service for our company, I understand the hourly rate will be _____ per hour plus expenses (i.e. photographs, lodging, meals out of town, and miscellaneous expenses as such). To begin the investigation, we hereby provide the following information, if available: (**Please include information for both client and his/her spouse, room-mate, girlfriend, boyfriend, etc., if applicable.**)

Name_____ AKA_____

Address_____ Previous_____

City_____ _____

State, ZIP_____ _____

DOB_____ _____

Social Security_____ _____

Height_____ _____

Weight_____ _____

Ethnicity_____ _____

Distinguishing Marks_____ Hair Color_____

Type of Claim_____ _____

Date of Injury_____ _____

Nature of Injury_____ _____

Employer_____ _____

Duties_____ _____

Vehicles_____ _____

Home Phone_____ _____

Restrictions_____ _____

Who Can ID?_____ _____

Represented By?_____ _____

Claim #_____ _____

Please supply any other information which will enable us to complete our investigation, i.e. limps, neck brace, etc.

In addition to our suppling a formal report, we request photographs plus_____ to help complete this claim.
Please do not spend more than _____ hours or _____ dollars on this claim.

_____
Company Name

_____
Address

_____
Phone

_____
Agent or Authorized Rep.

_____
Company Attorney

_____
Date

Cobra Company
"When no one else cares"

File Name_____Claim #_____Pg #____

Investigator 1_____Investigator 2_____

DAY	DATE	TIME	DETAILS

ABOUT THE AUTHOR

Bob Bruno was trained in investigation and surveillance by the U.S. government in 1965 under the army's CID command during his enlistment in the U.S. Marine Corps. He was an undercover drug investigator for two years. His last year was spent in Vietnam in Marine Corps Force Reconnaissance. His eight-month tour included more than 2,000 hours of surveillance in the jungles surrounding Khe Sanh. He was wounded three times and medevac'ed before the end of his normal thirteen-month tour of duty.

Bruno and three others would exit base camp in the still of darkness, hump a couple of miles through the bush, and set up surveillance. Each man was responsible for watching a north, south, east, or west sector. If enemy movement was detected, a call to headquarters resulted in the battleship *New Jersey* sending off a few rounds from her sixteen-inch guns, while standing a few miles offshore. Air support was often called in. All of this firepower was controlled by four young Recon marines *doing surveillance* deep in the cover of the bush. It kind of gets in your blood after a while.

After leaving the Marine Corps, Bruno began working in the private sector, doing (what else?) surveillance. Today he owns and operates a PI firm called Cobra Company. Its primary work is surveillance.